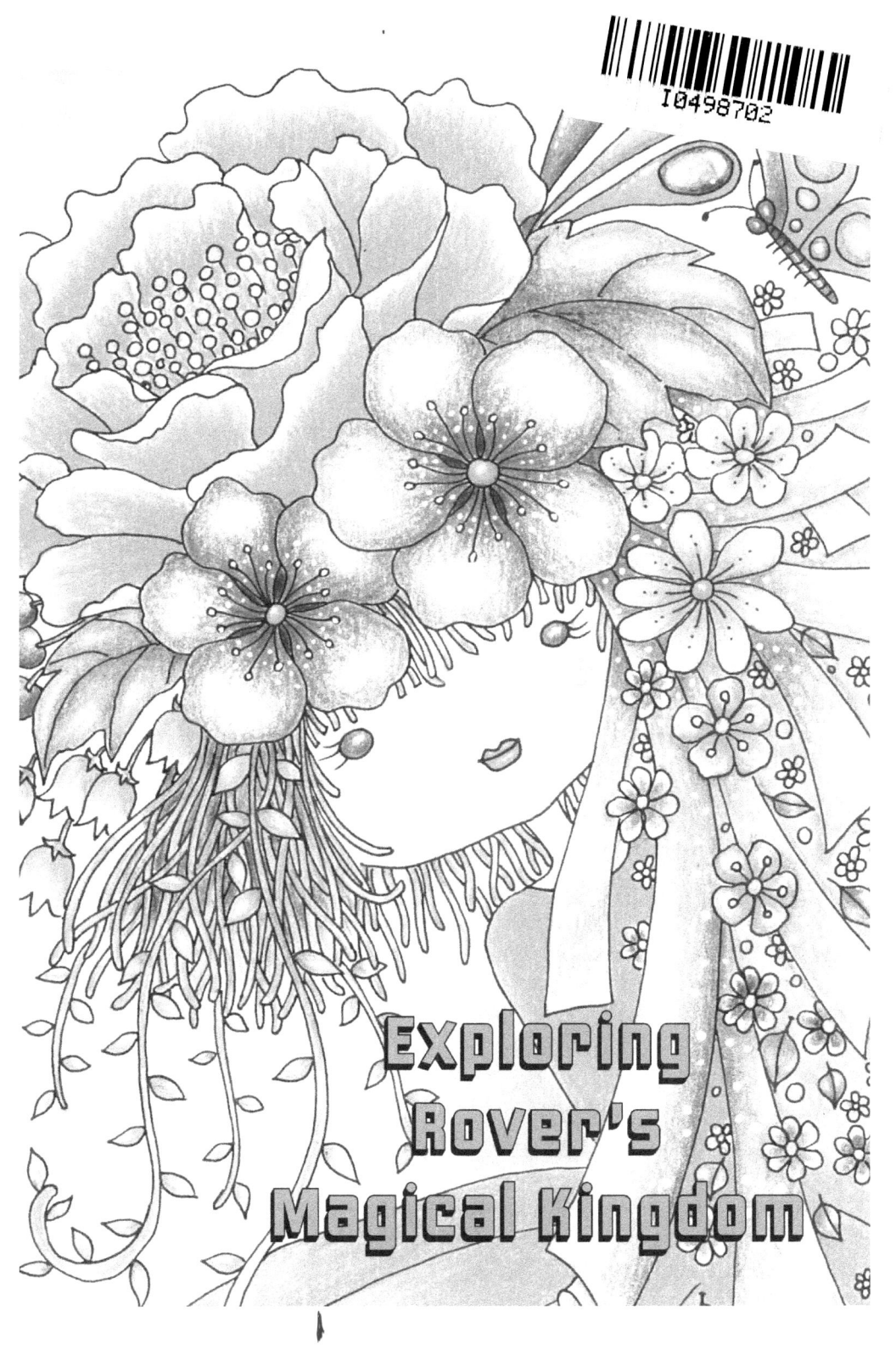

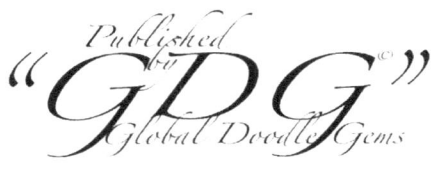

Share your colored versions with us ! We love seeing your results

and hearing from you

we are social !

The Official FB book page, stay on top of what we have in the works !
www.facebook.com/globaldoodlegems
The Community group, share your colored pages, meet the artists, enjoy exclusive freebies, take
part in community Charity books and so much more......
www.facebook.com/groups/globaldoodlegems/
Follow us on Twitter.... @GlobalDoodlegem
We are on Instagram too
@globaldoodlegems for instagram
...and if you are not social like that we have a blog
globaldoodlegems.wordpress.com

Copyright © 2017 Global Doodle Gems
All rights are reserved by Global Doodle Gems.
Duplication of pages for personal use are allowed. You are invited to color the pages then scan/post
your coloured versions to social networks, mentioning the book title and author/artist (Global Doodle
Gems).
All artwork and images are protected by copyright laws. This book or any portion thereof may not,
otherwise, be reproduced and/or distributed or transmitted without the express written permission of
the artist/publisher of Global Doodle Gems.
All of us from the Global Doodle Gems wish you a colortastic time and look forward to seeing your
wonderful color results online !

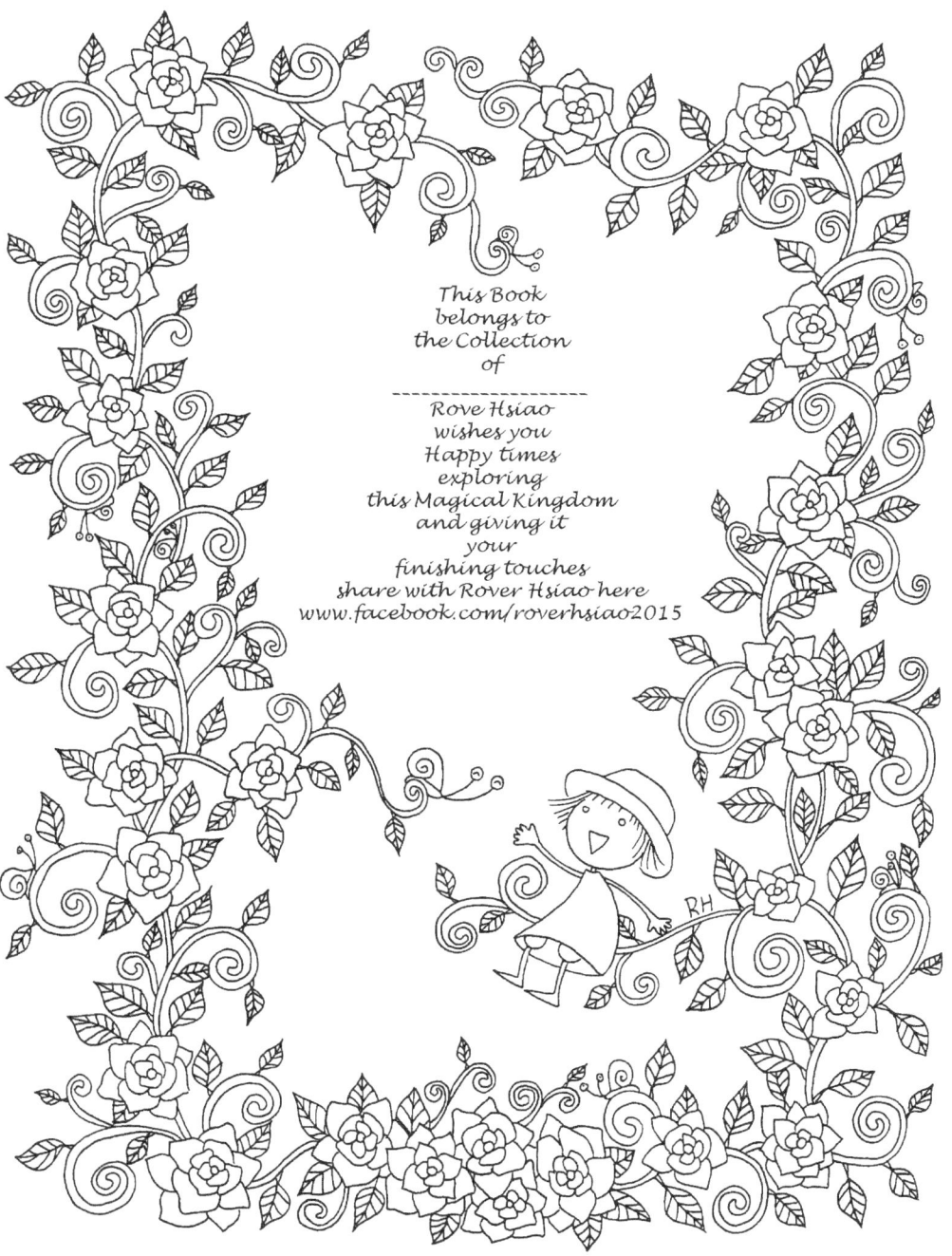

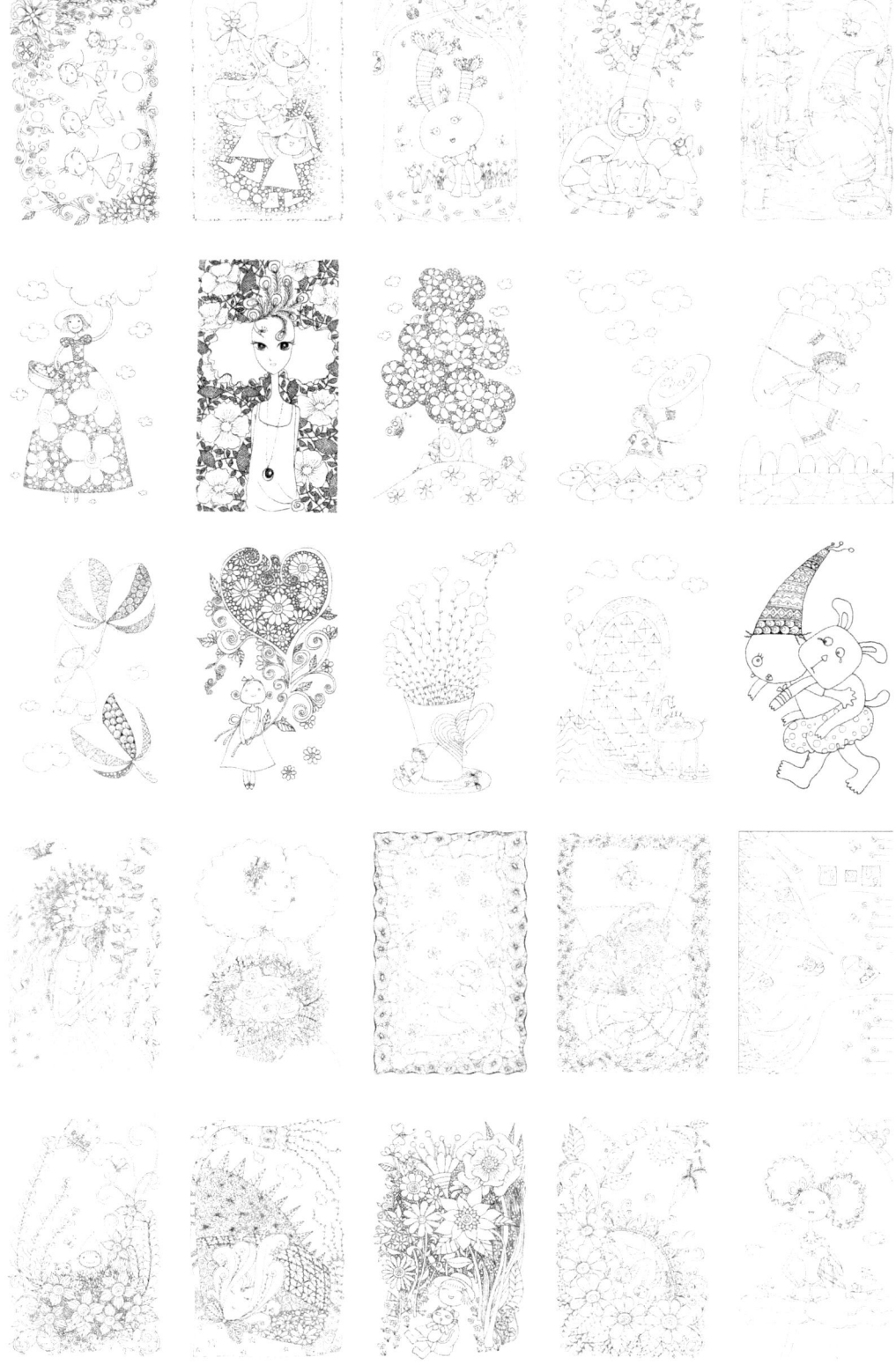

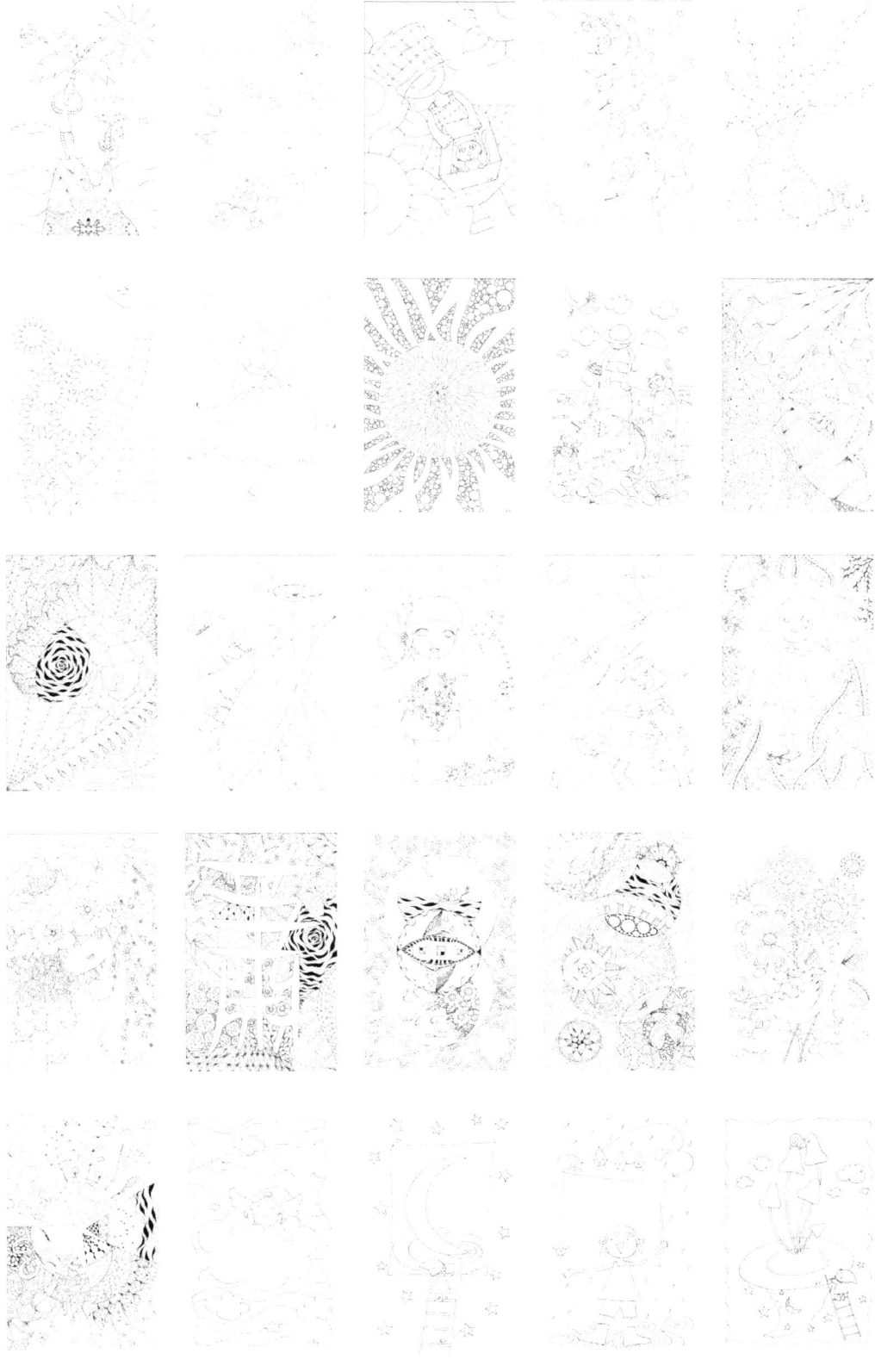

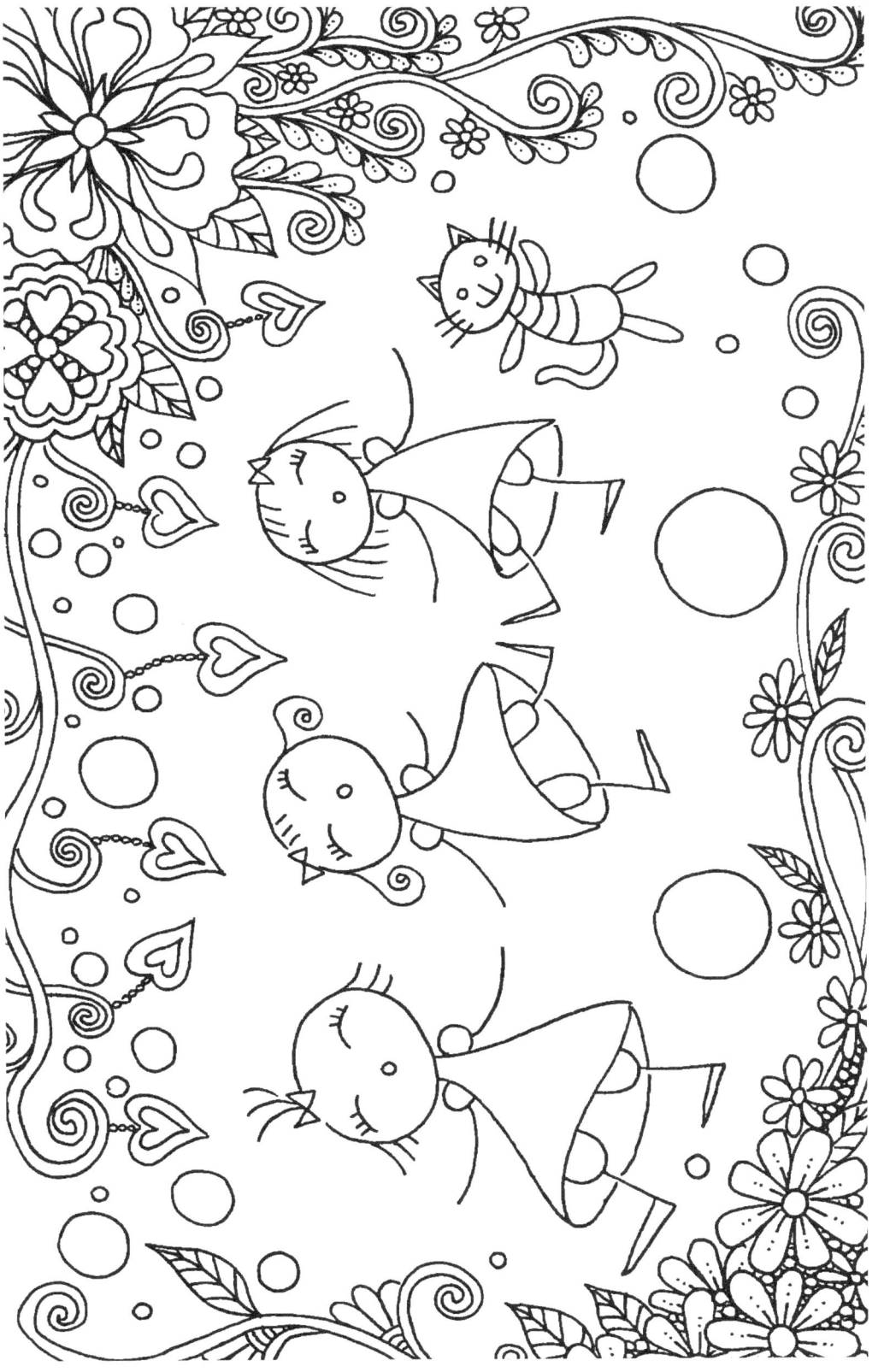

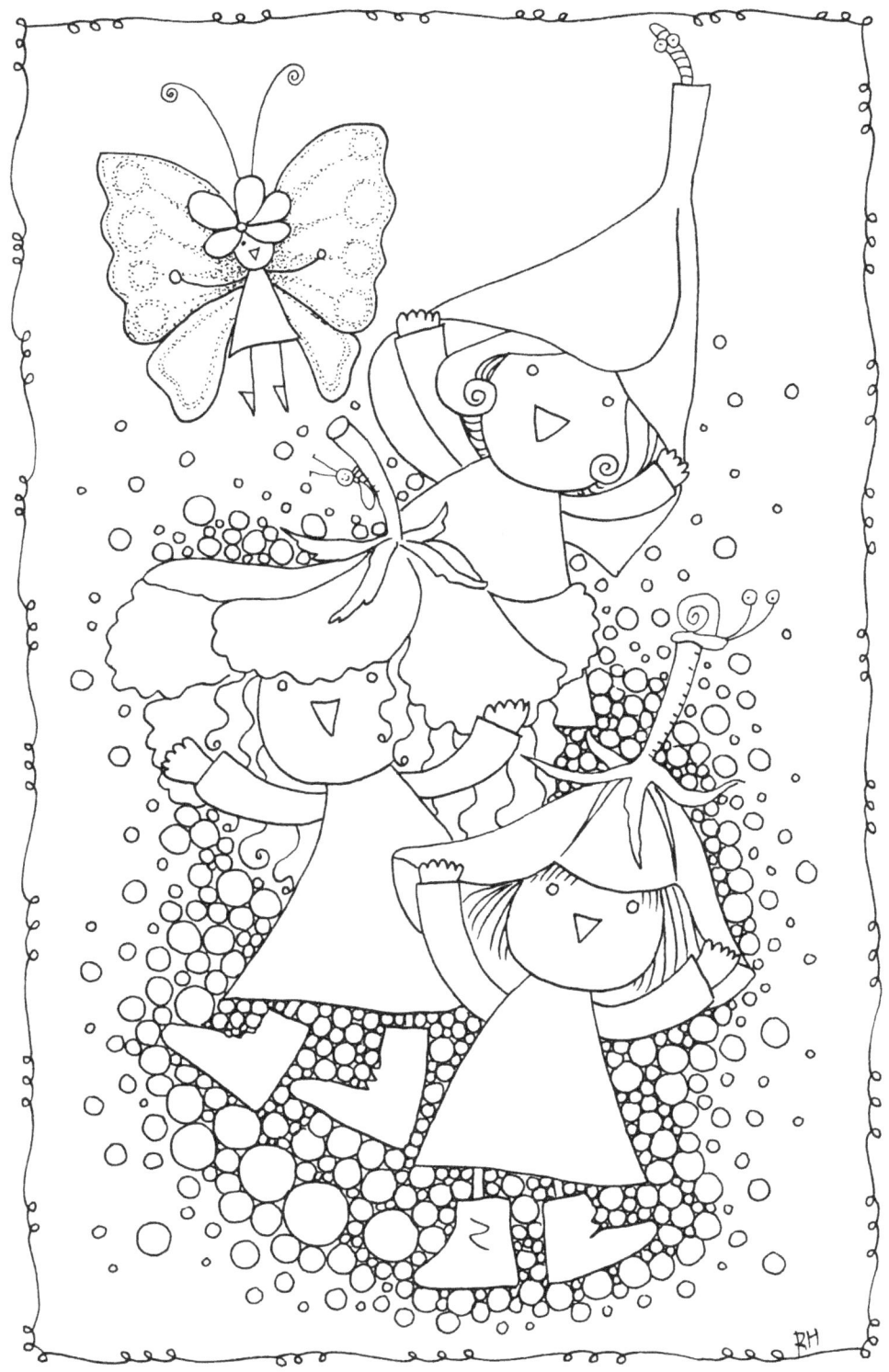

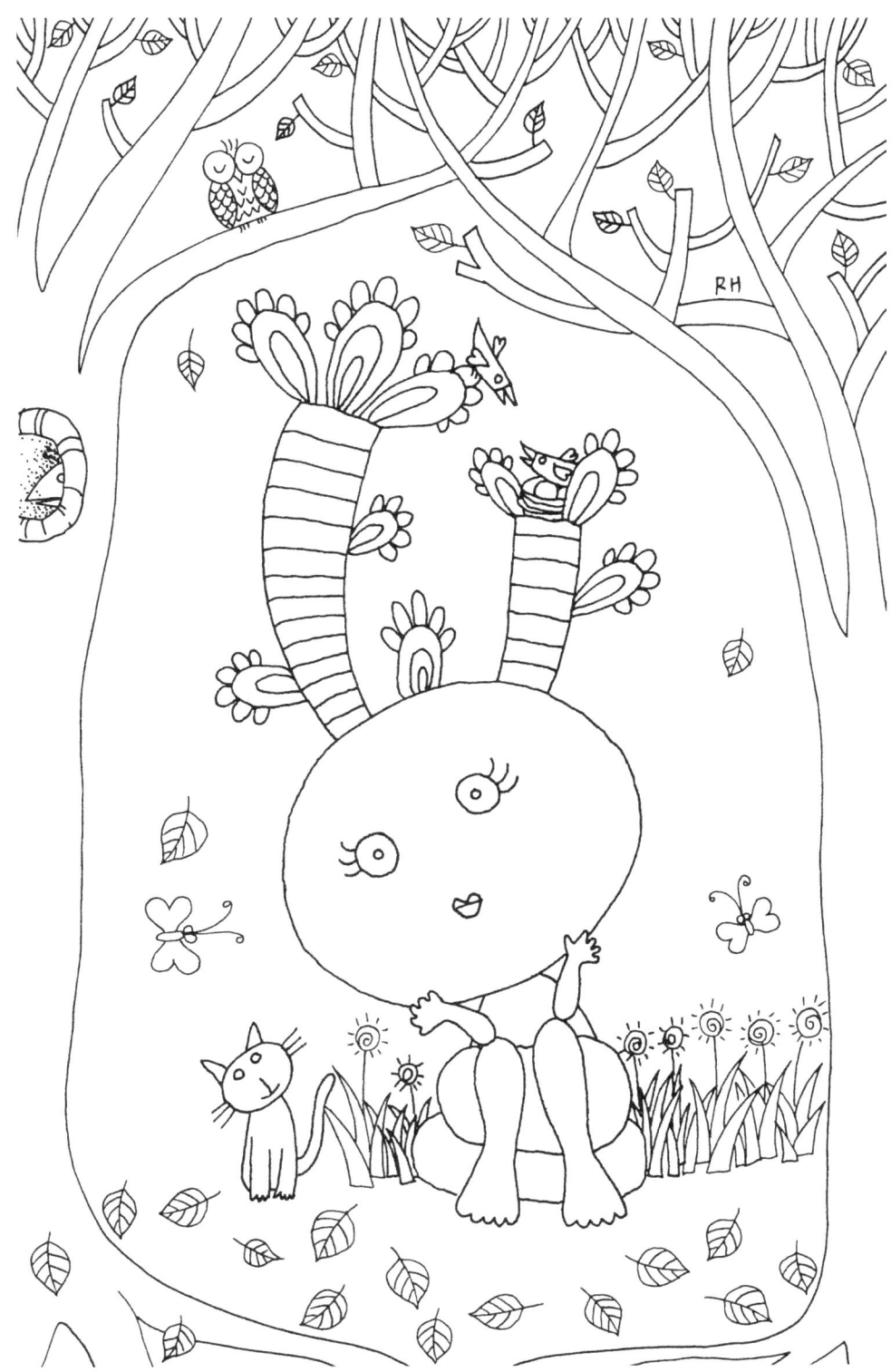

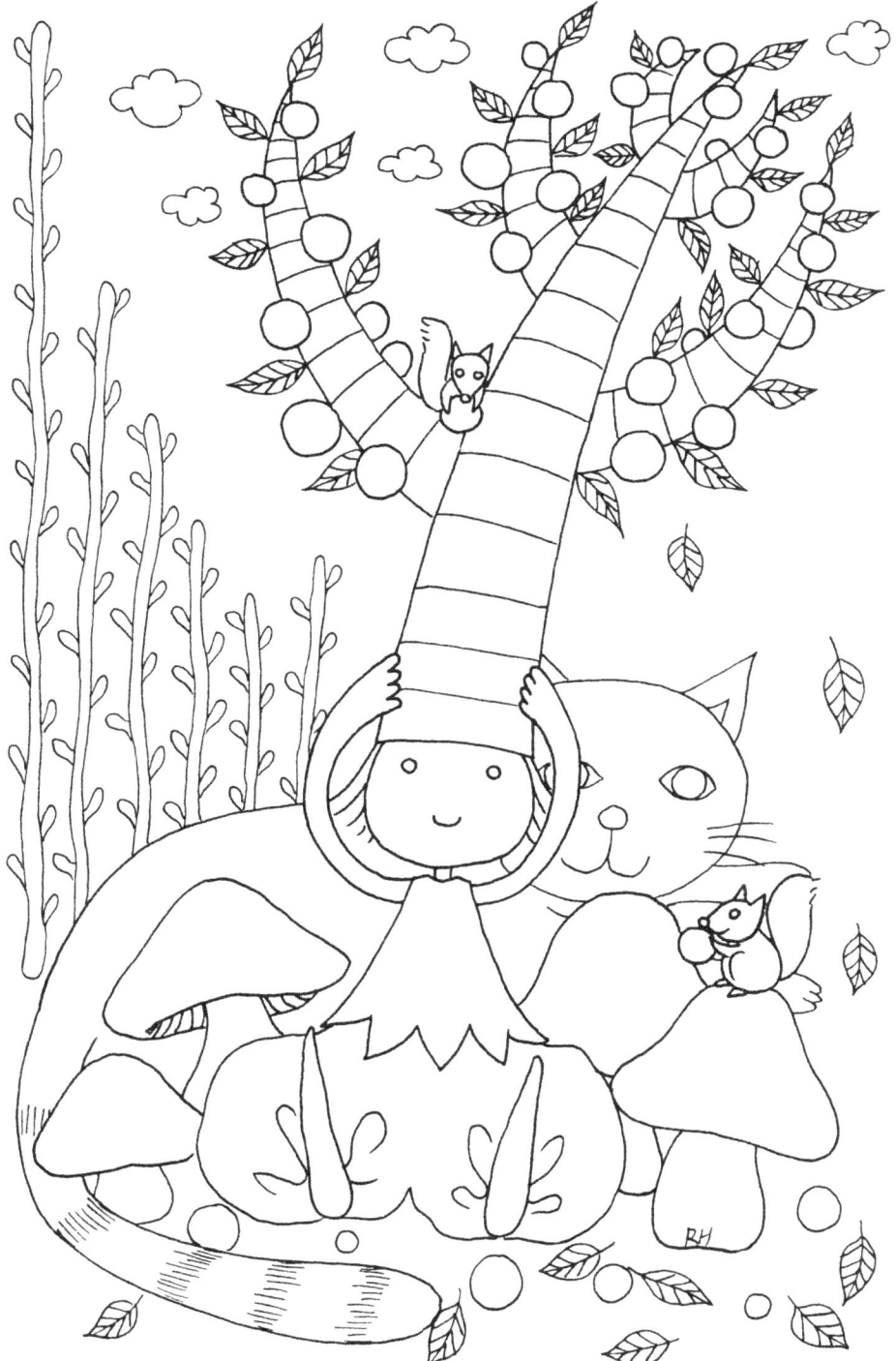

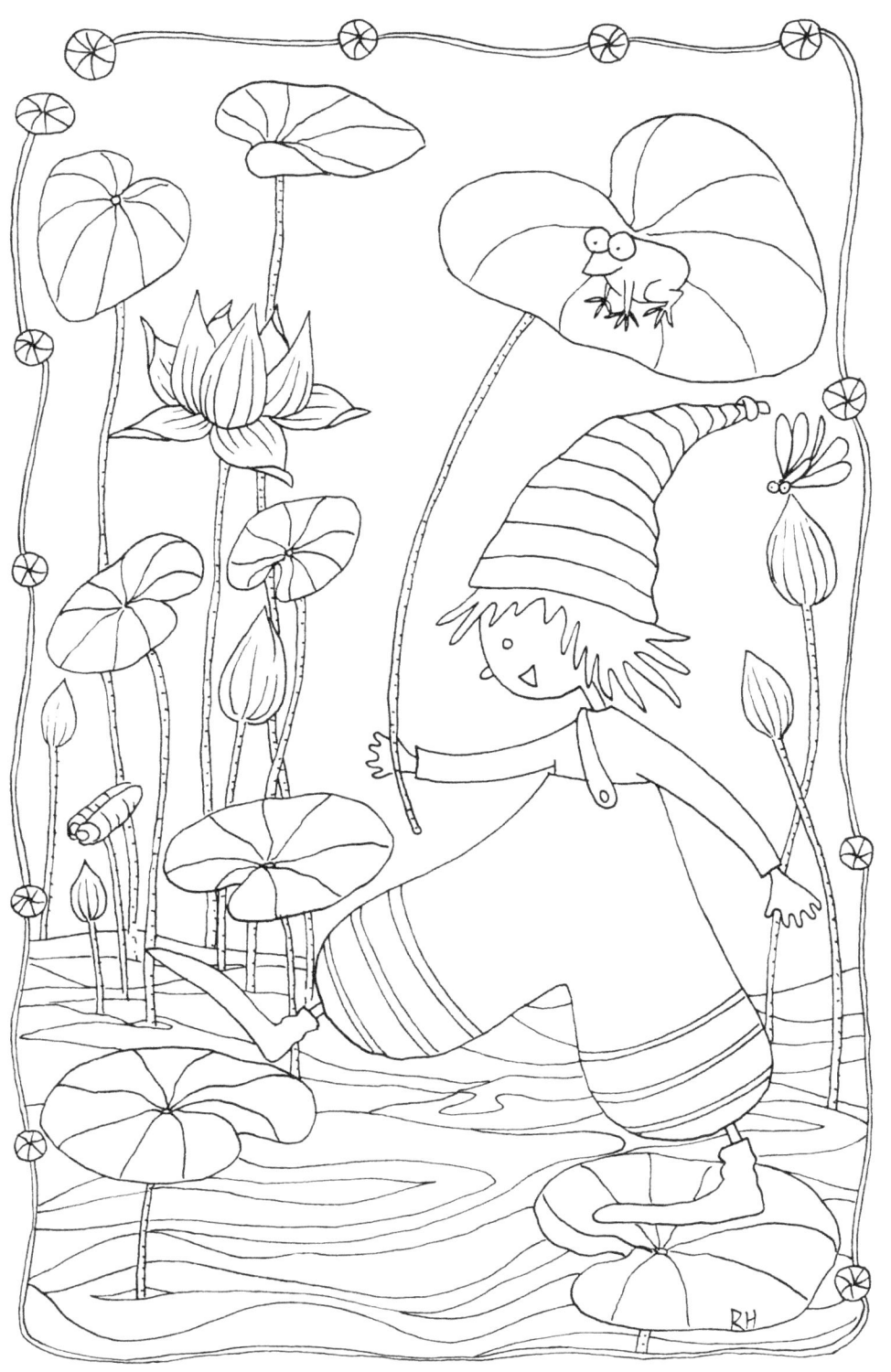

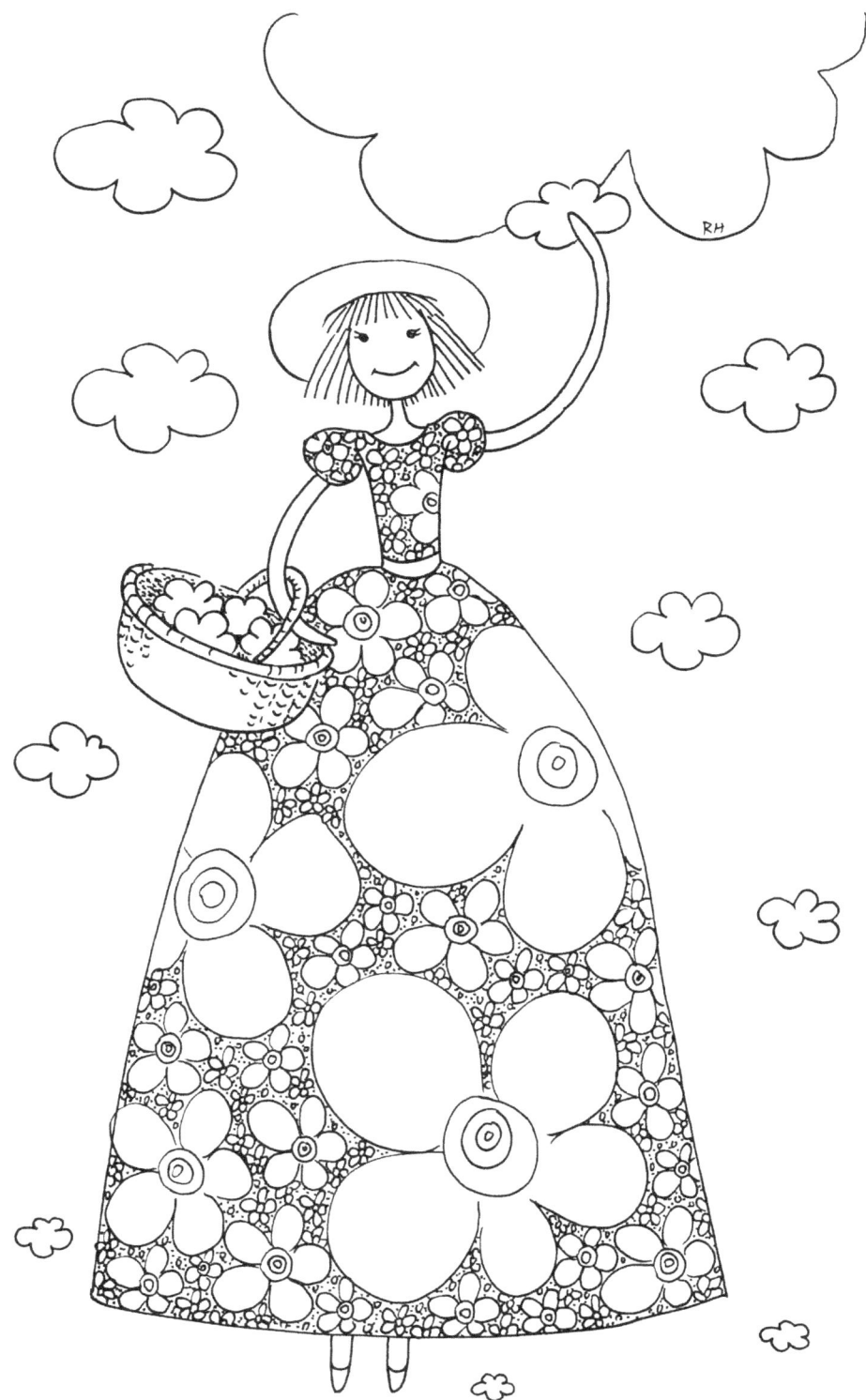

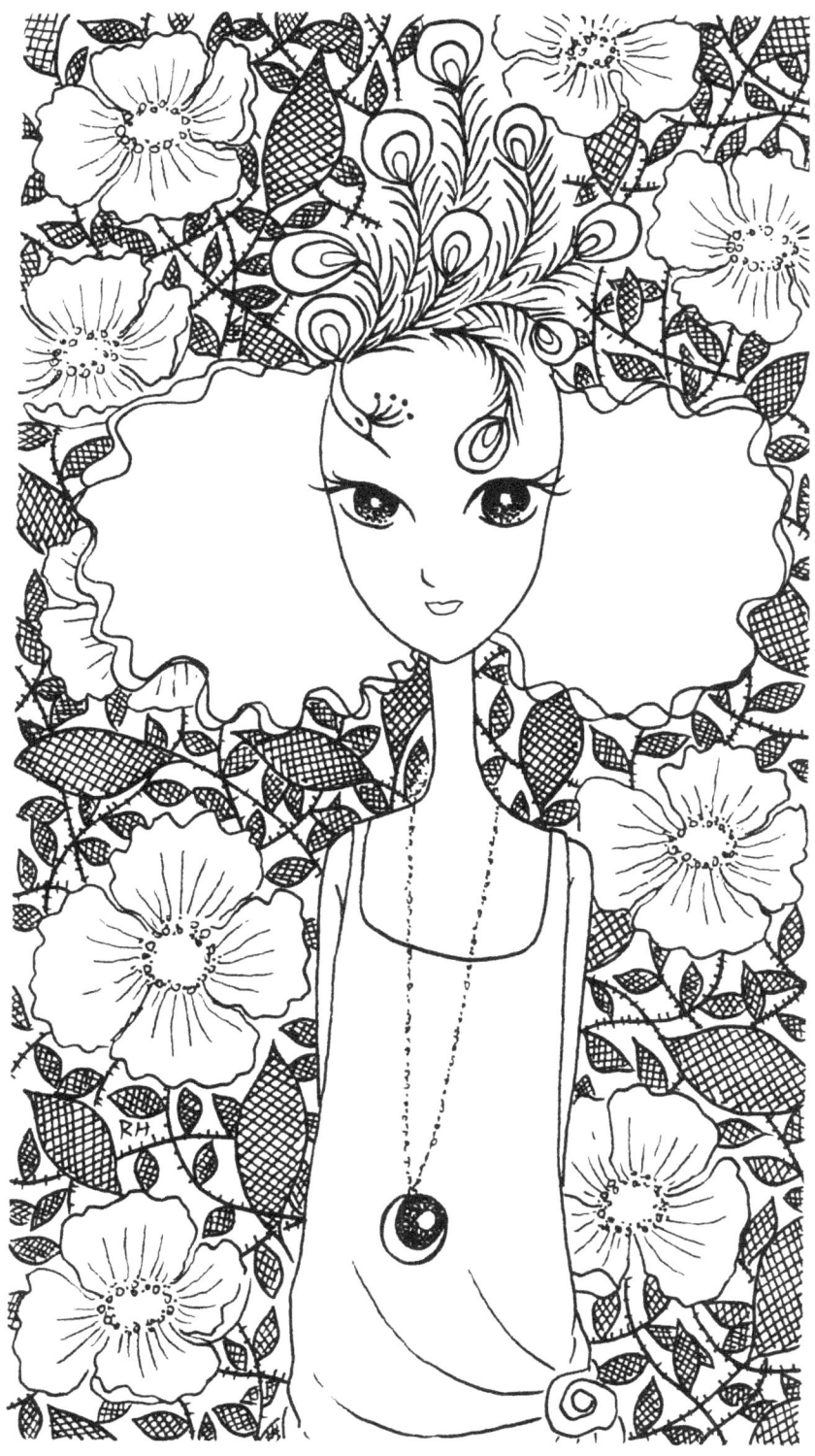

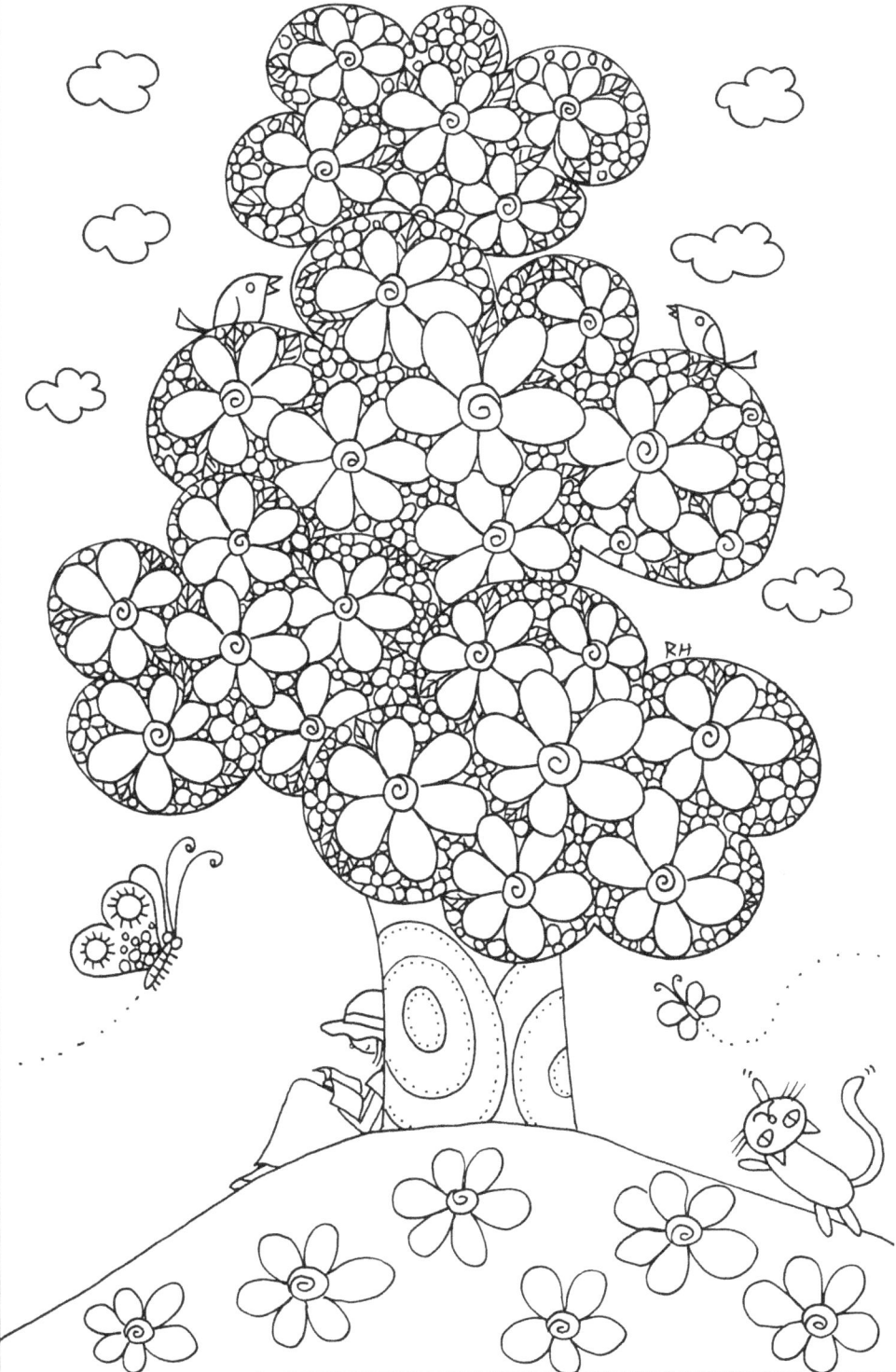

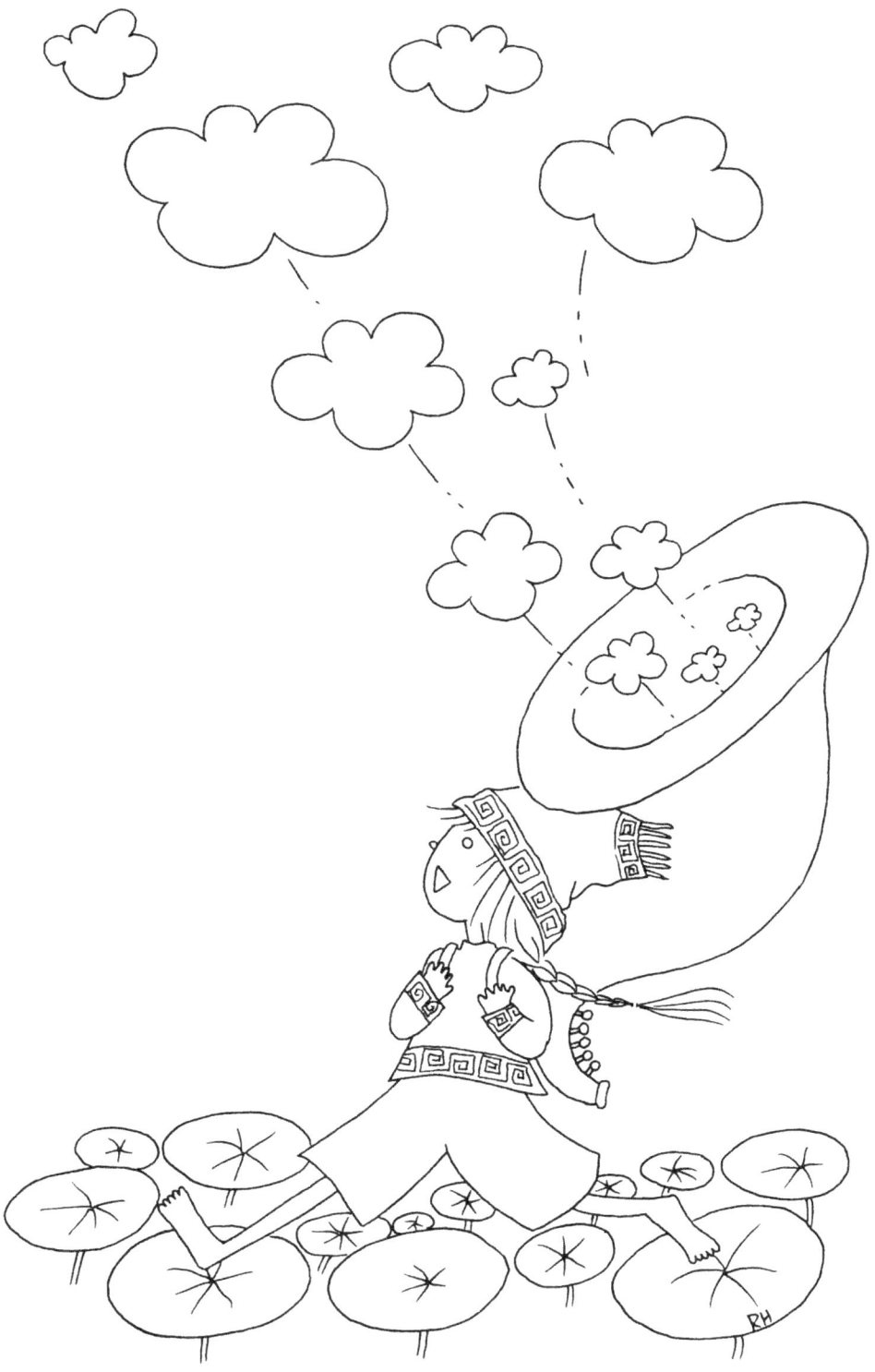

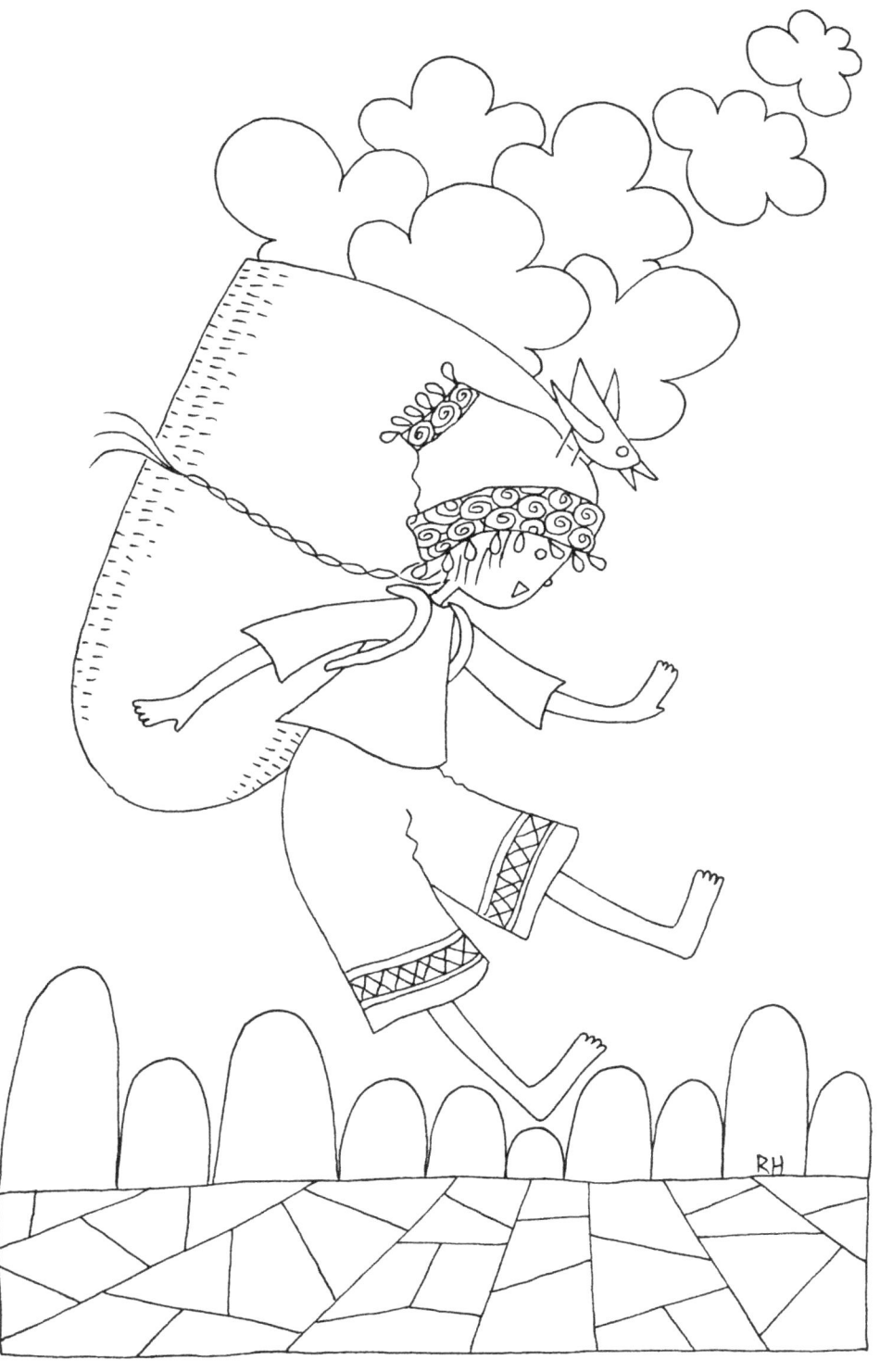

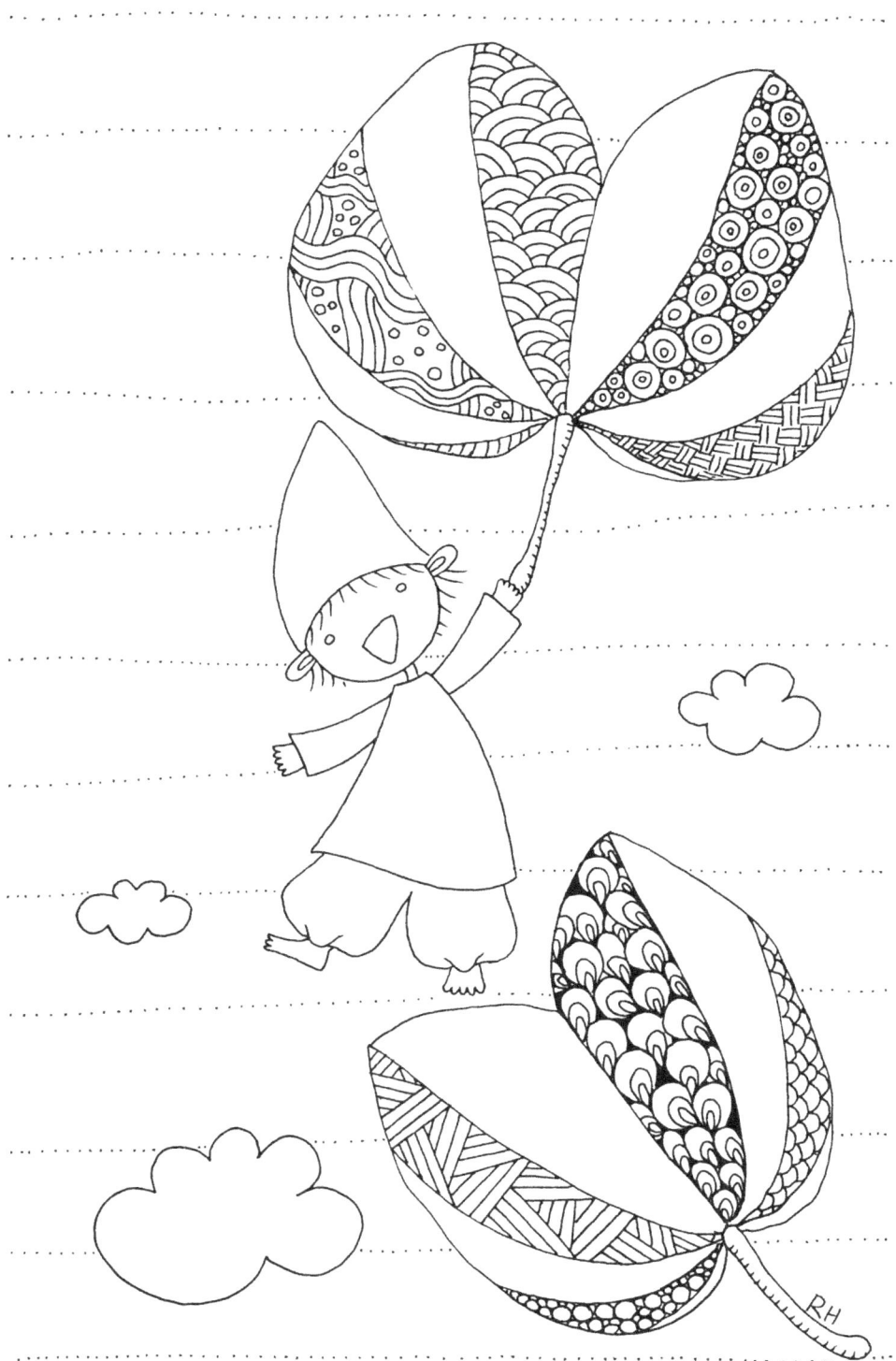

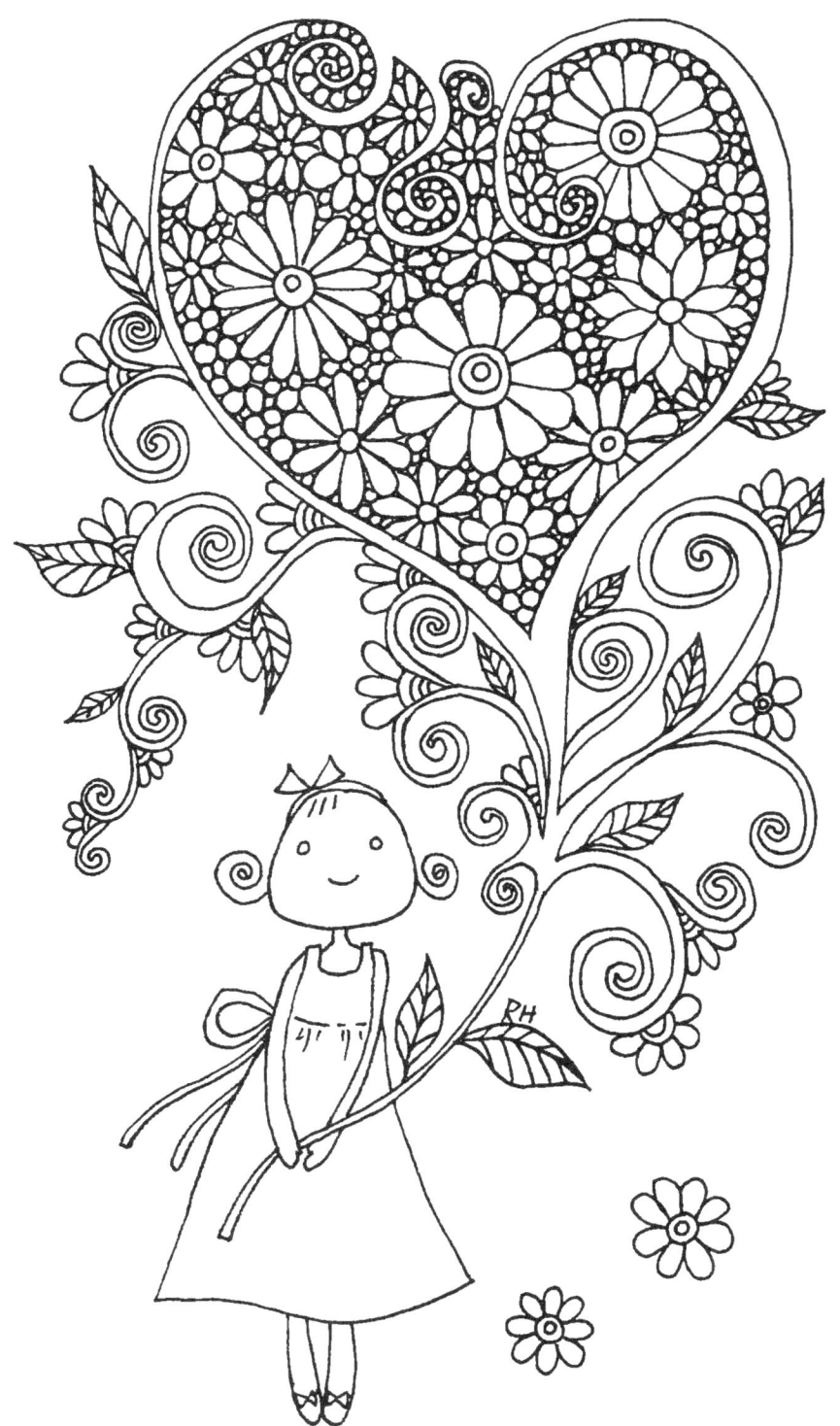

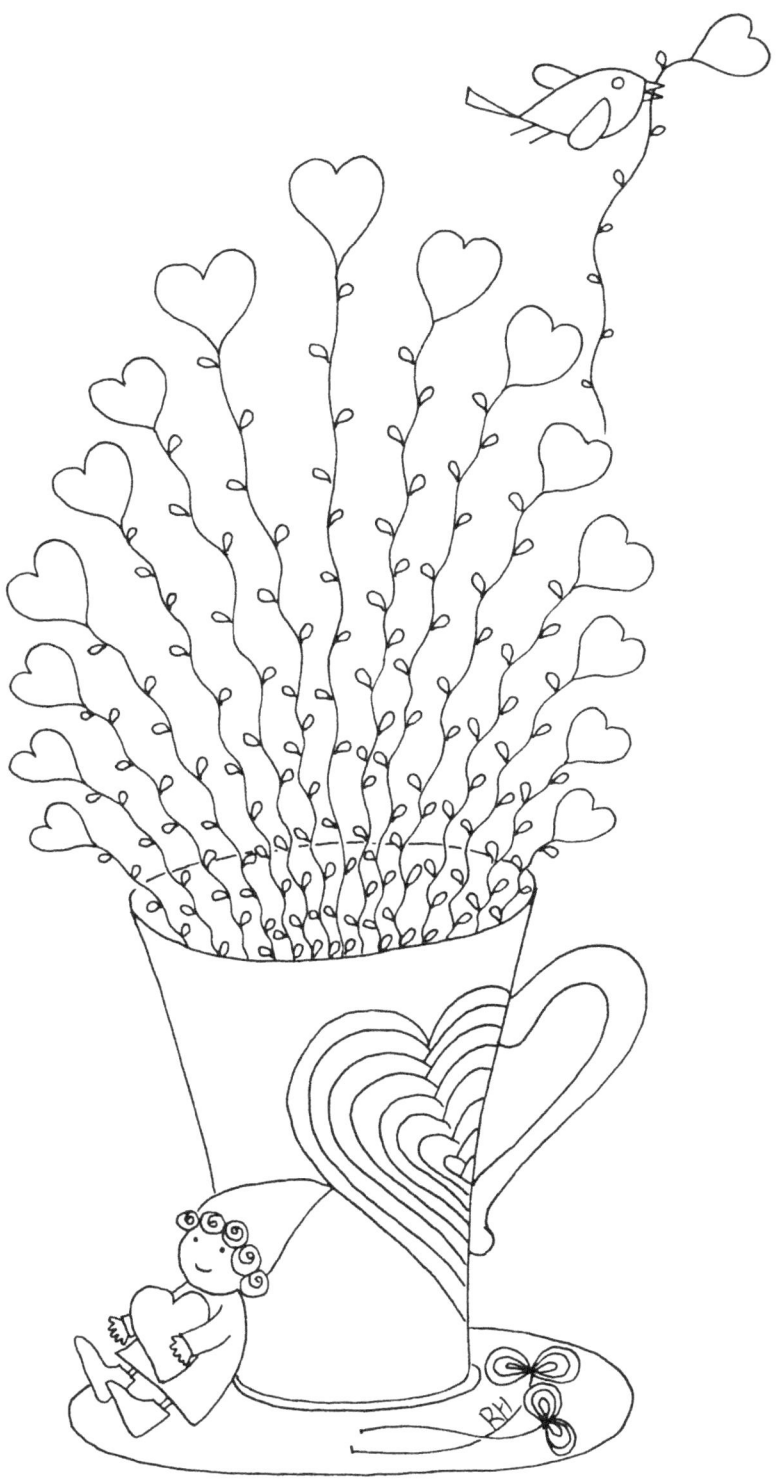

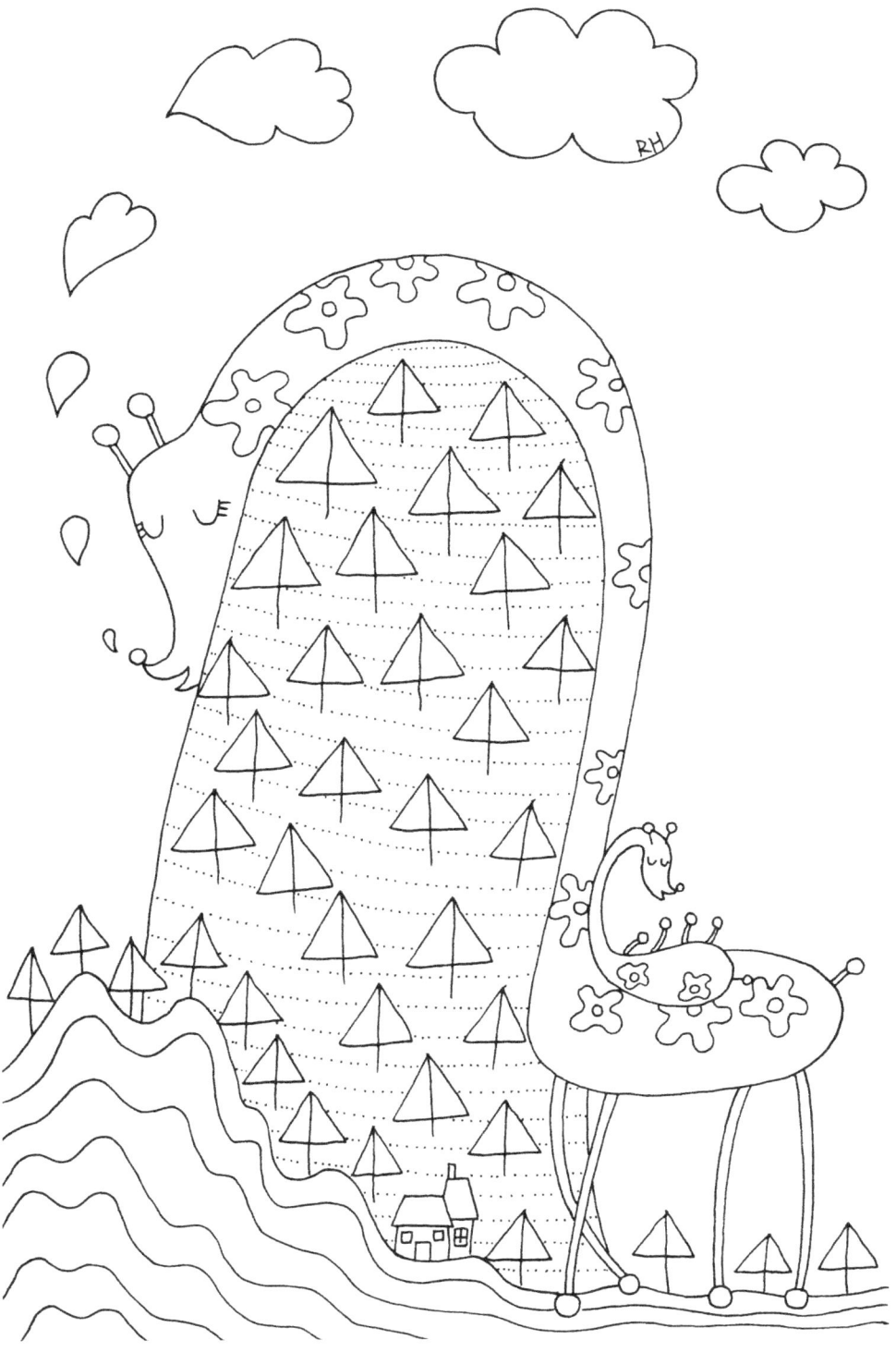

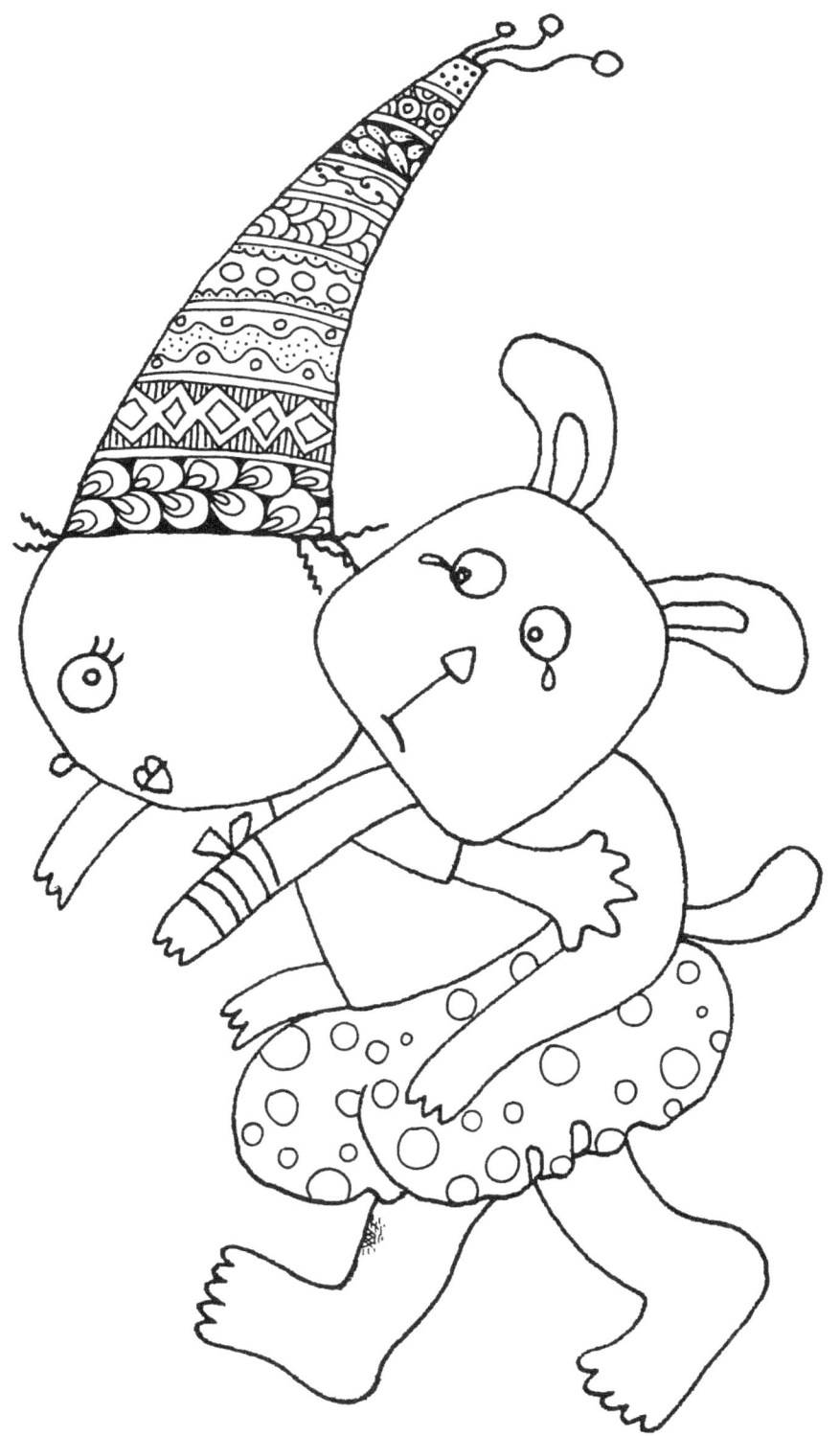

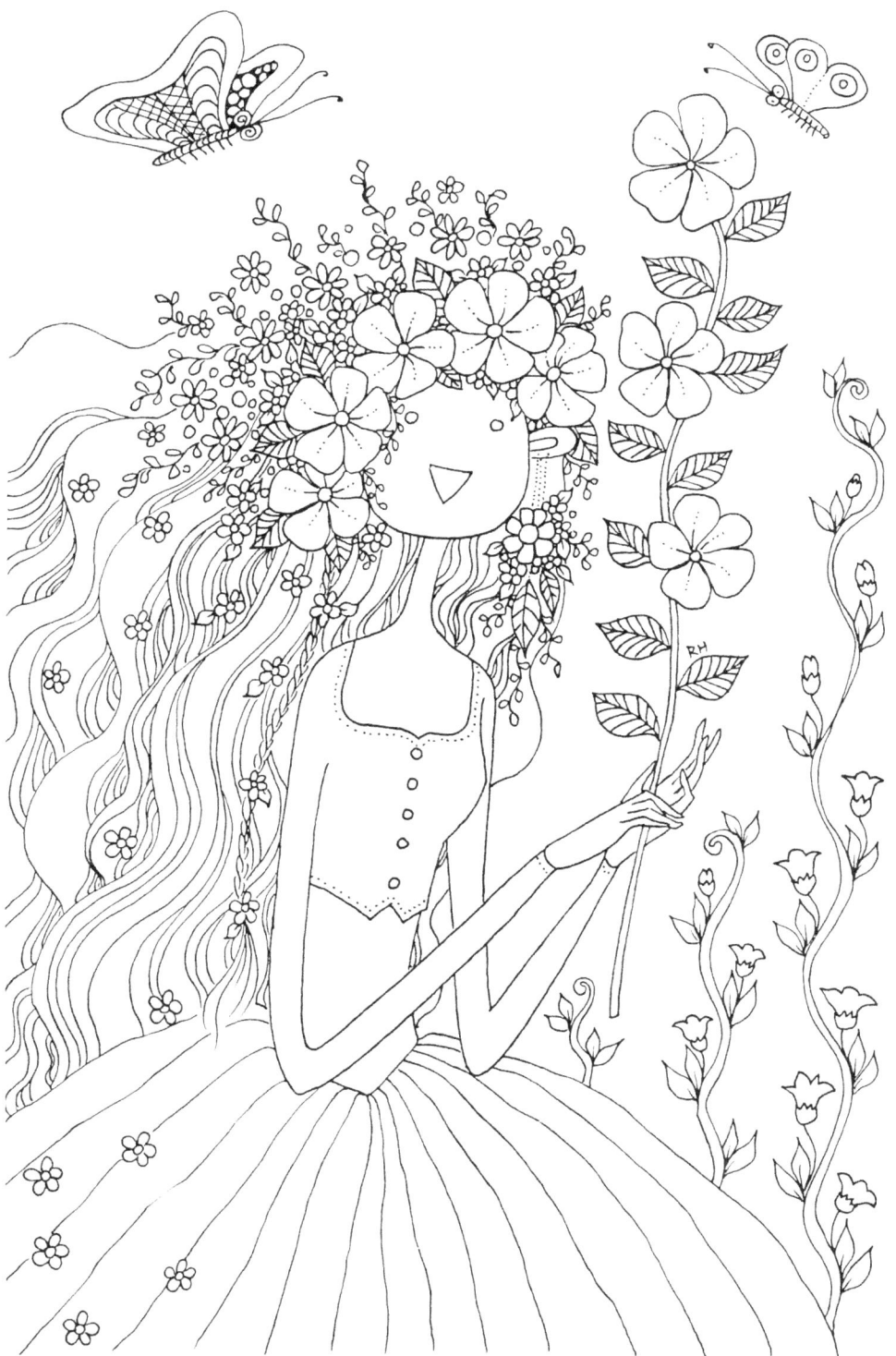

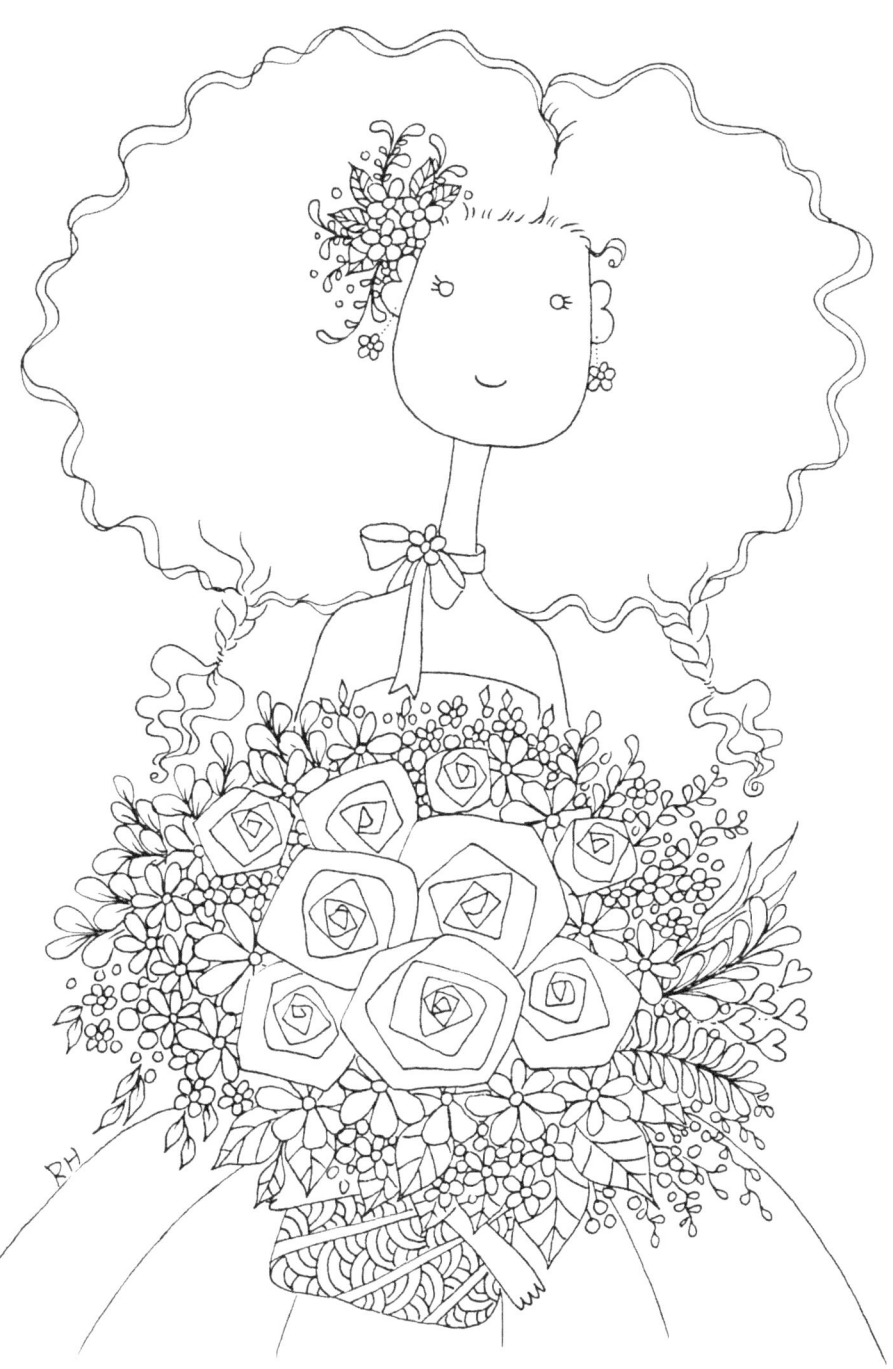

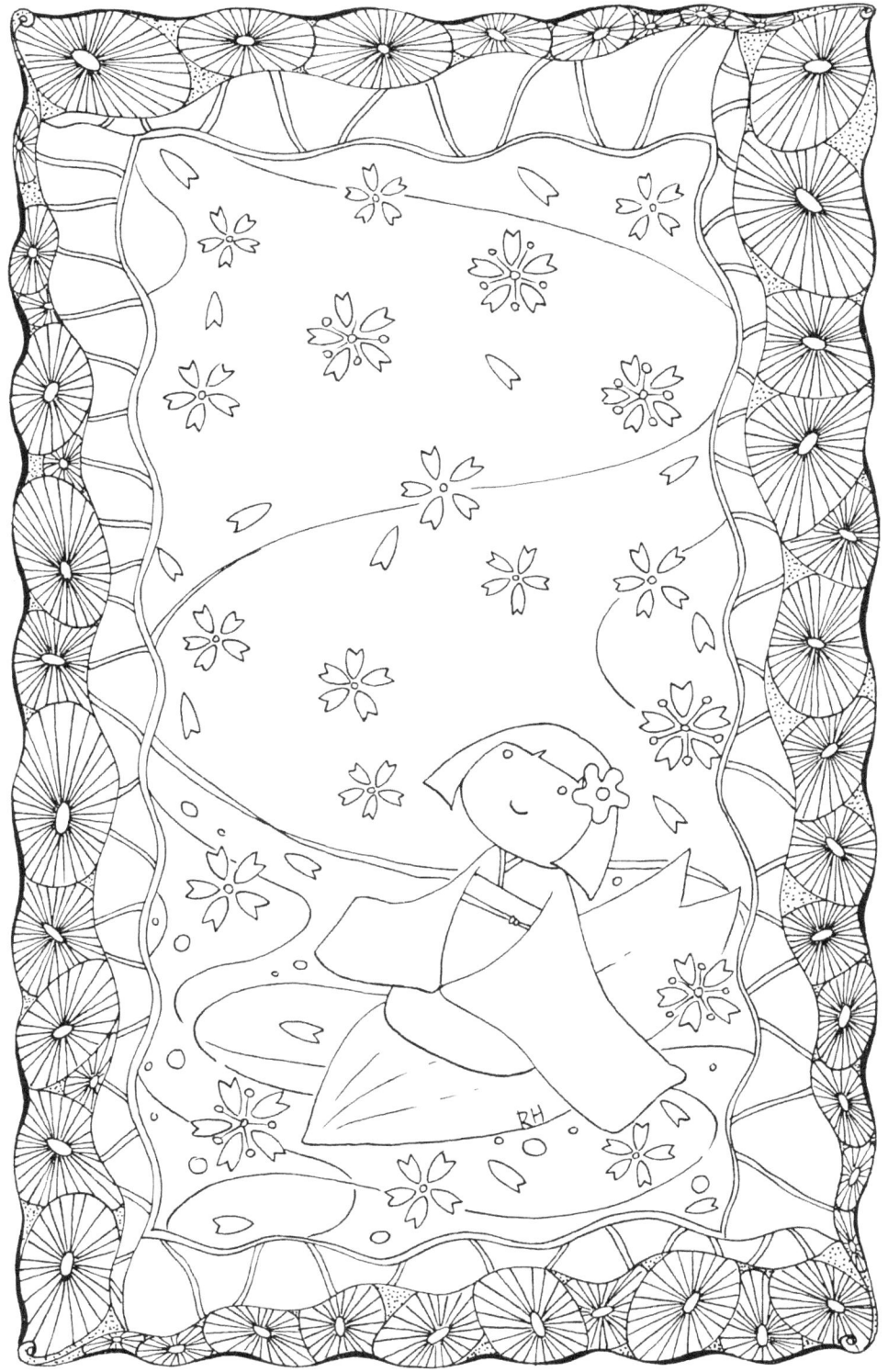

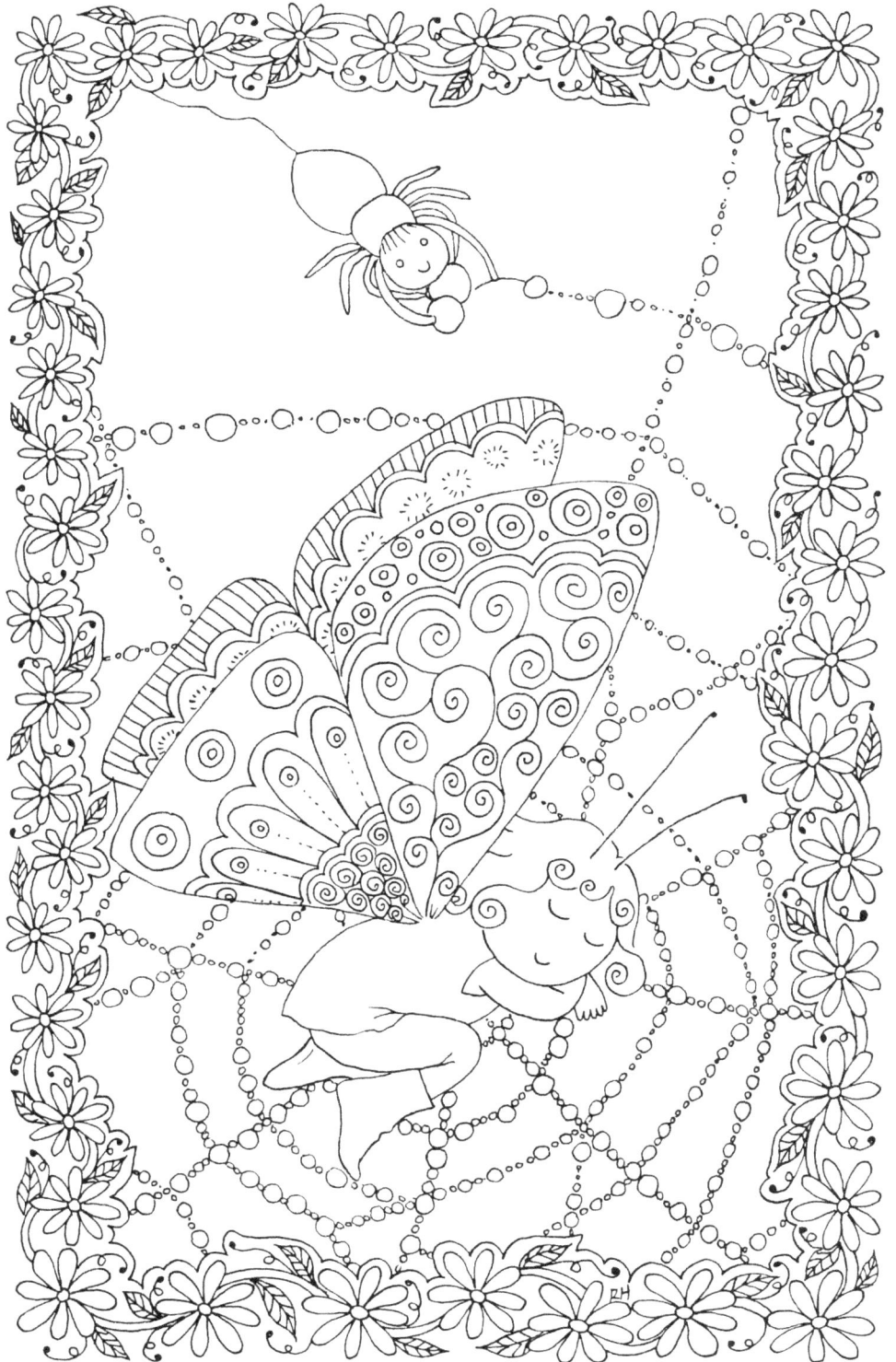

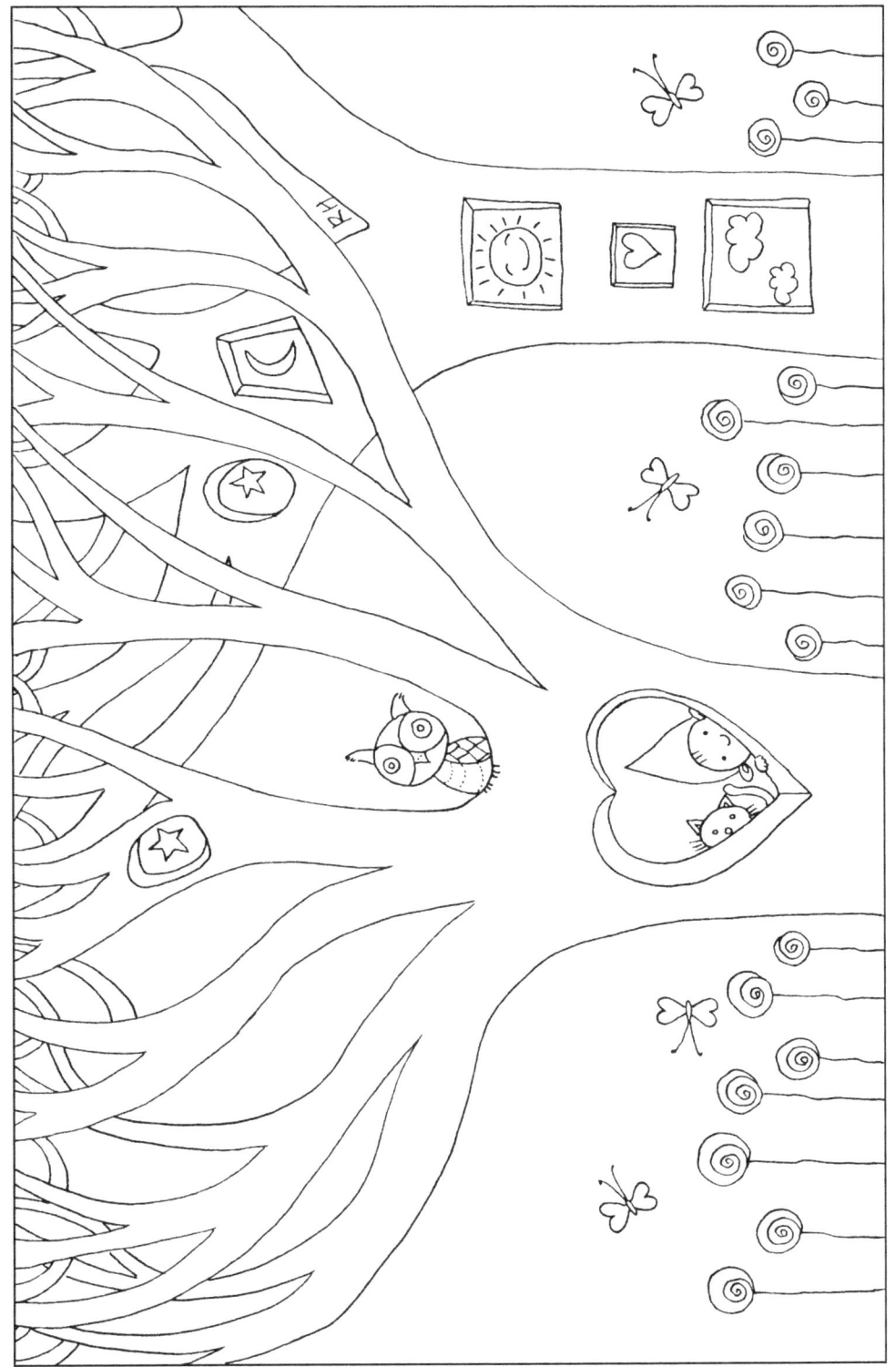

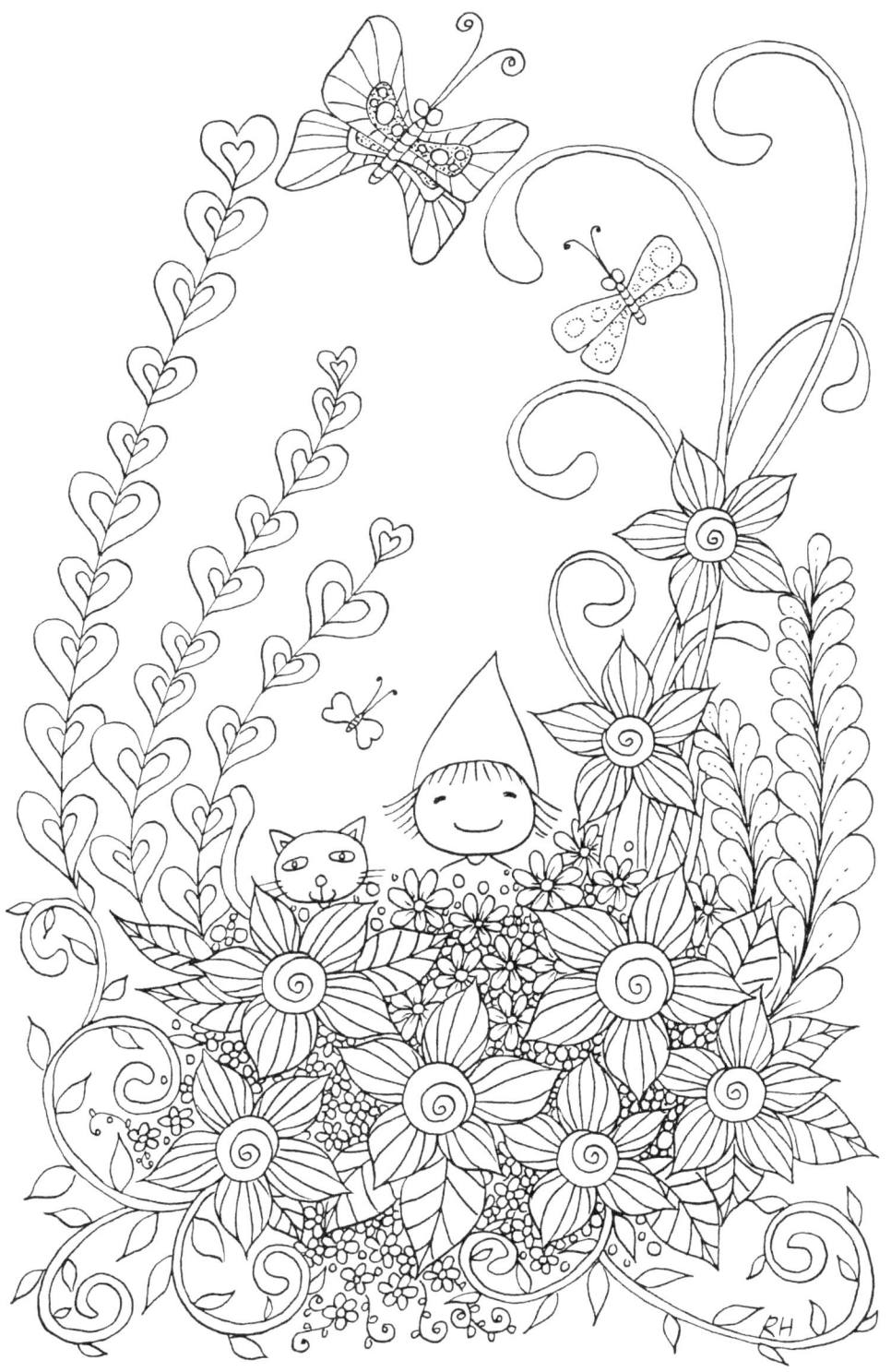

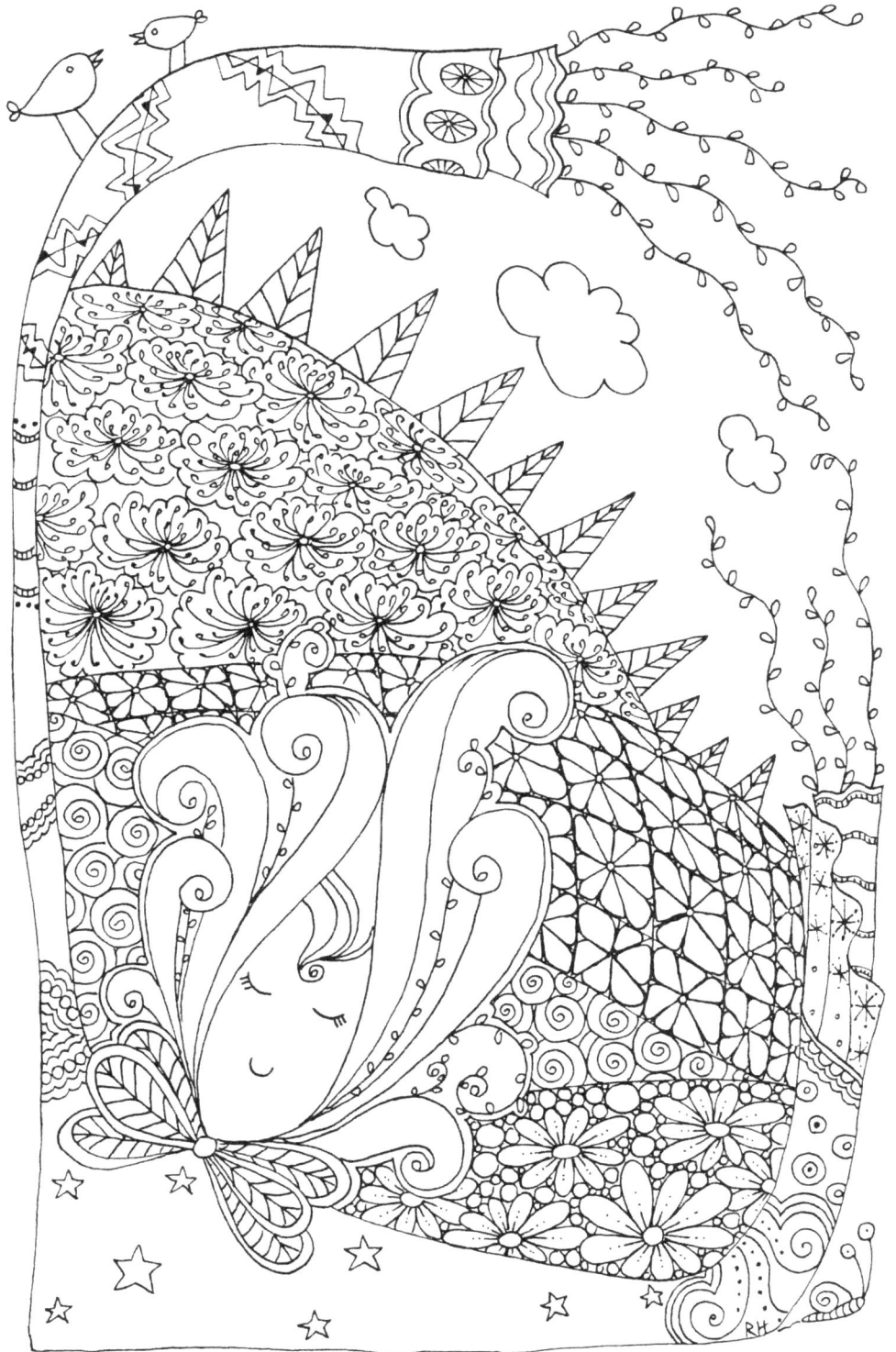

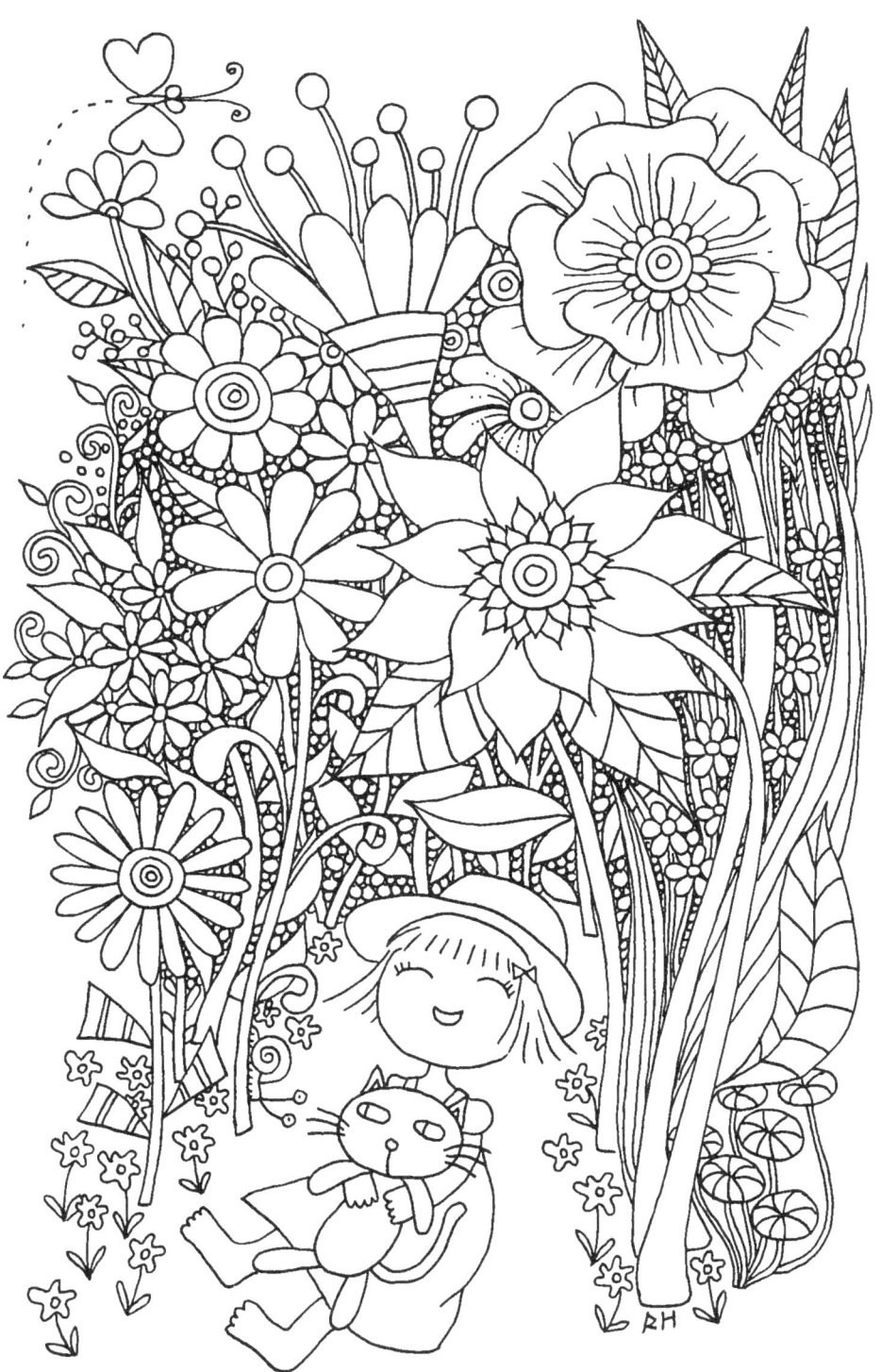

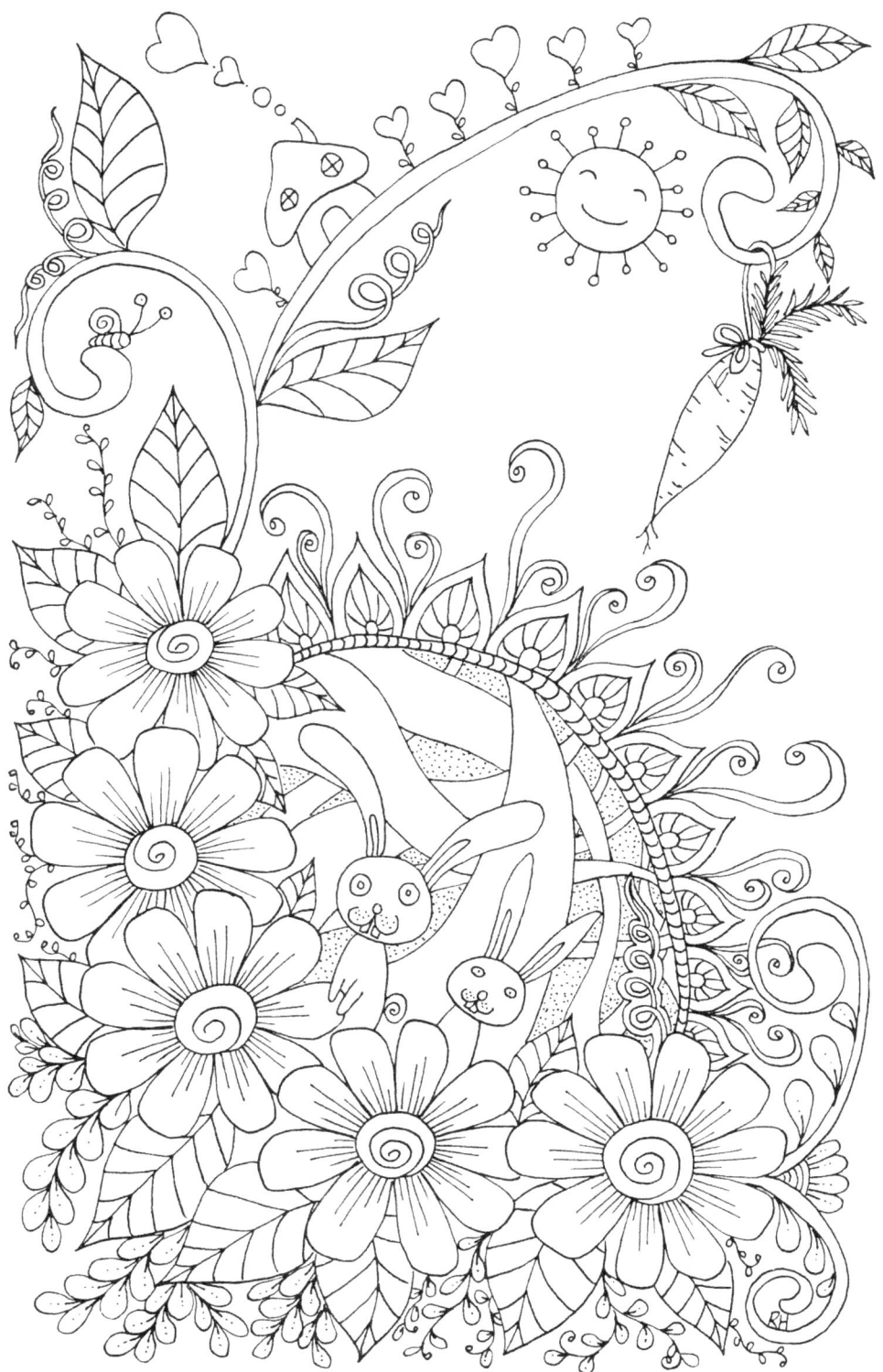

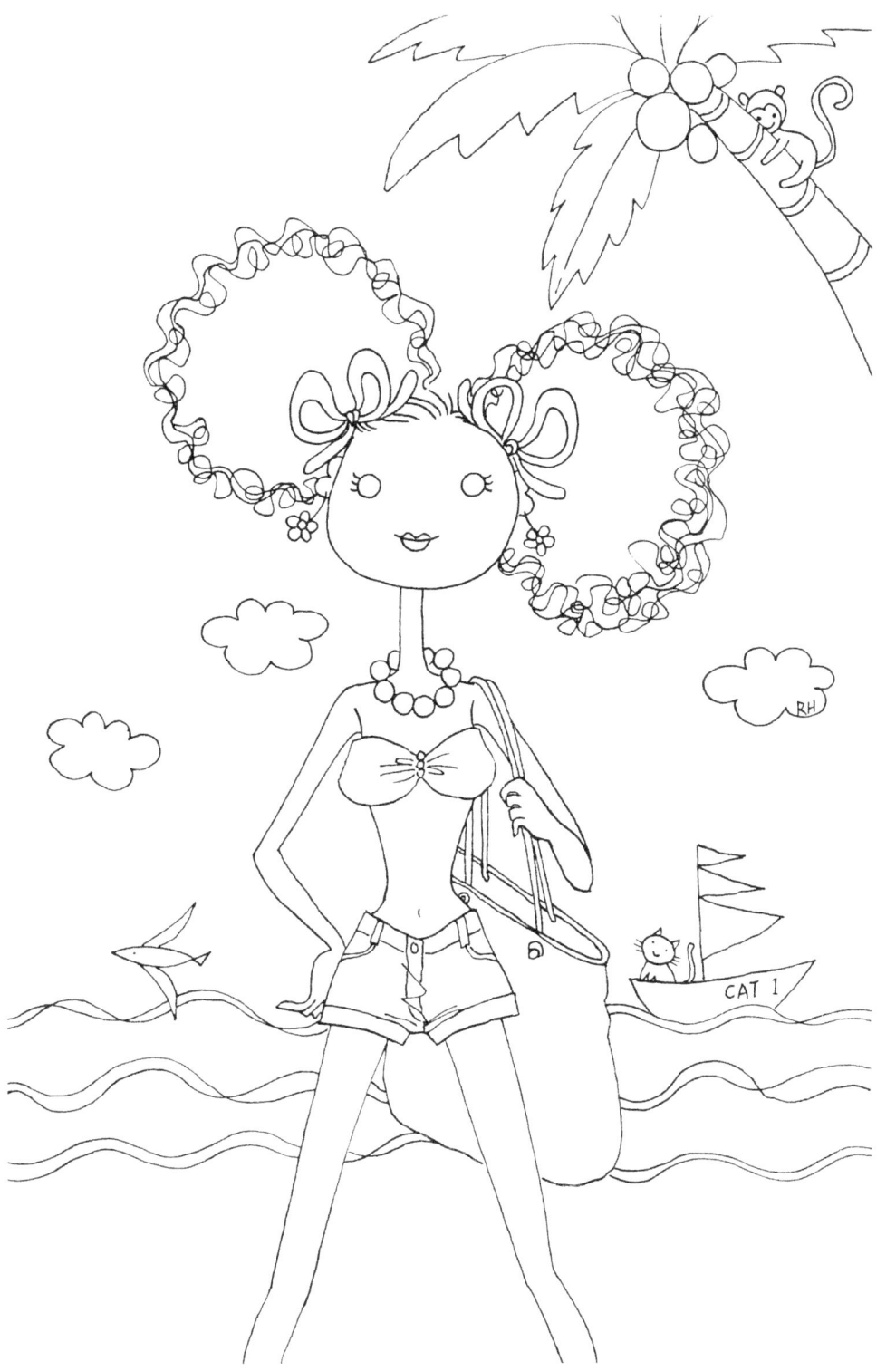

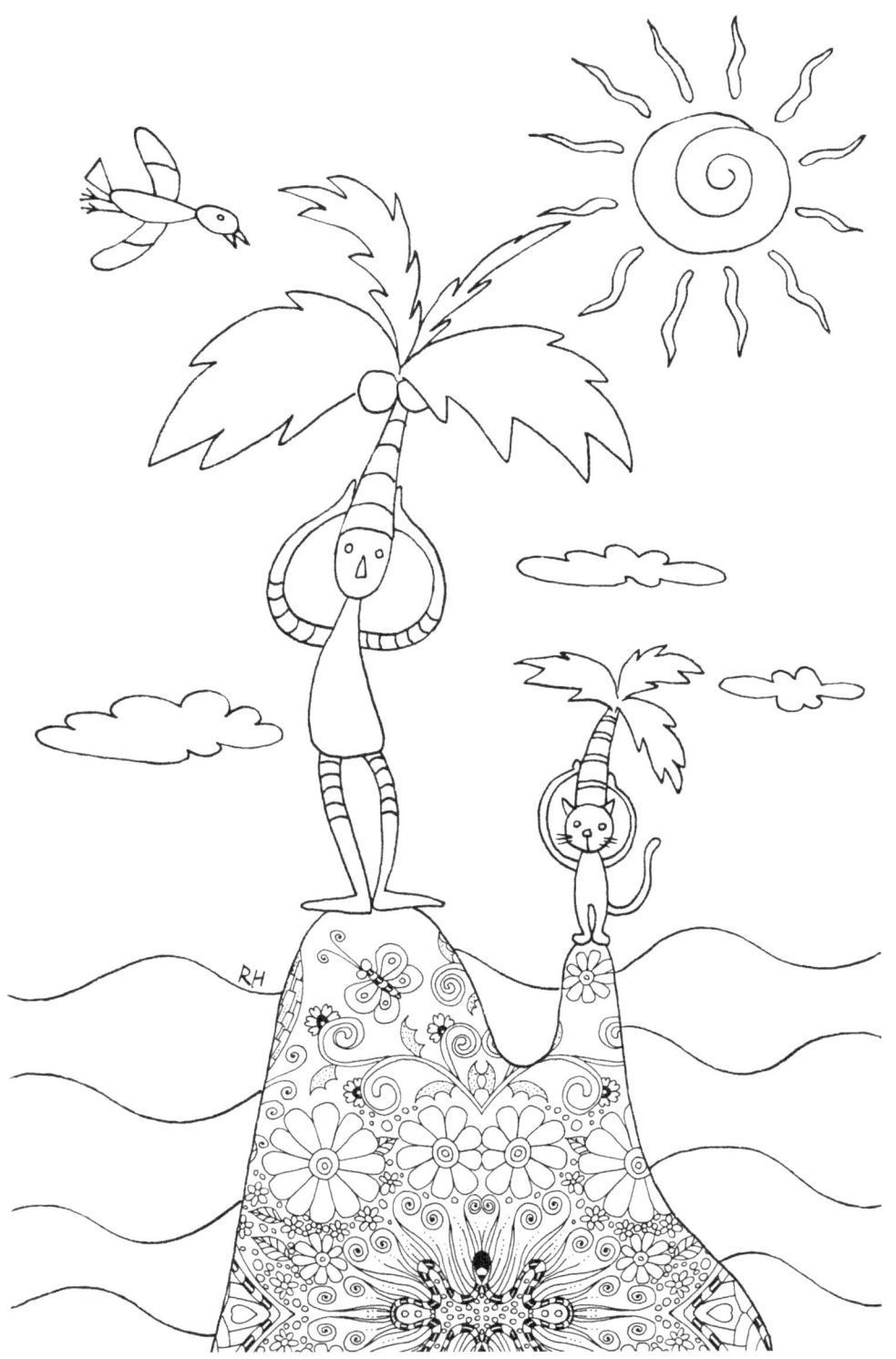

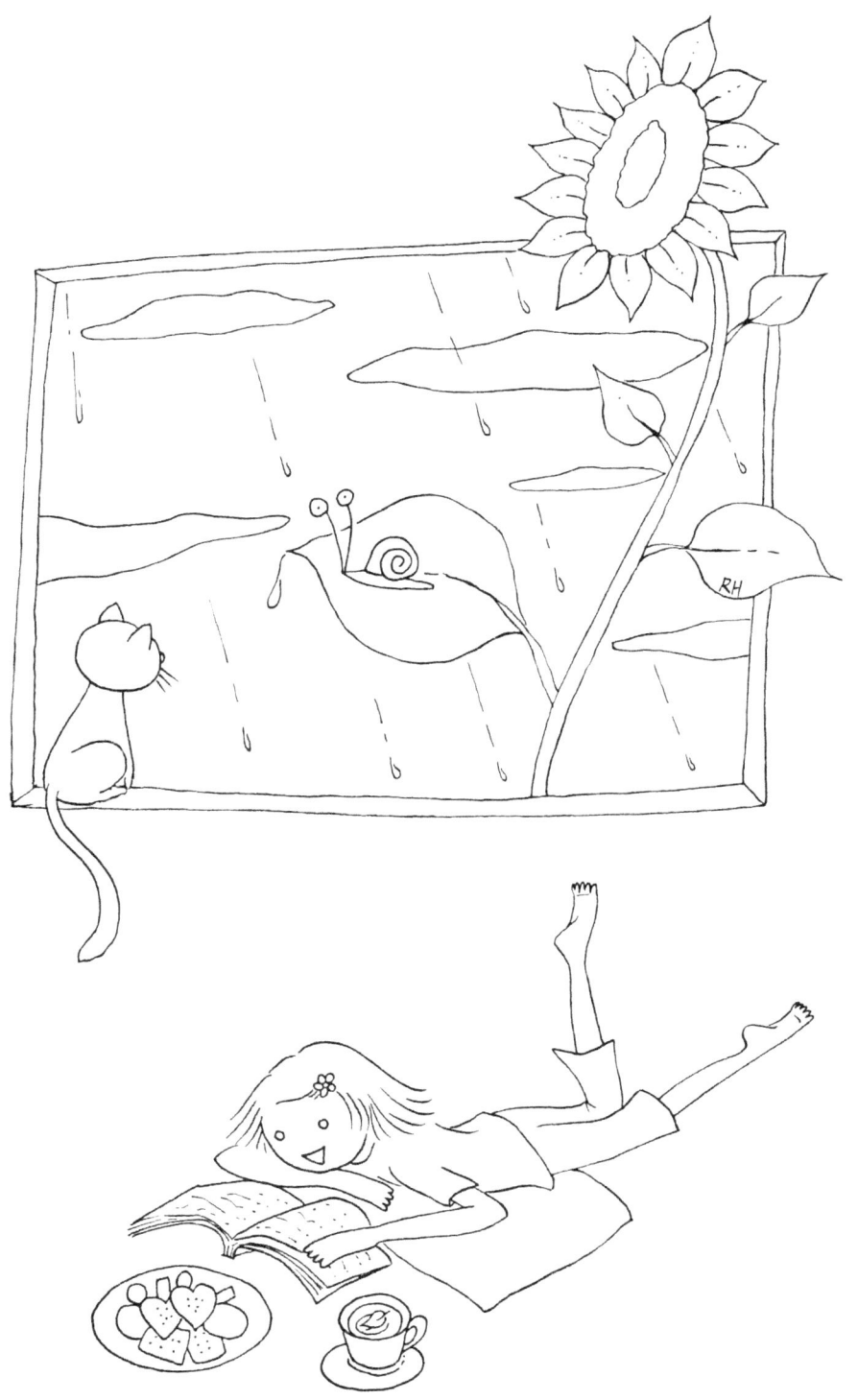

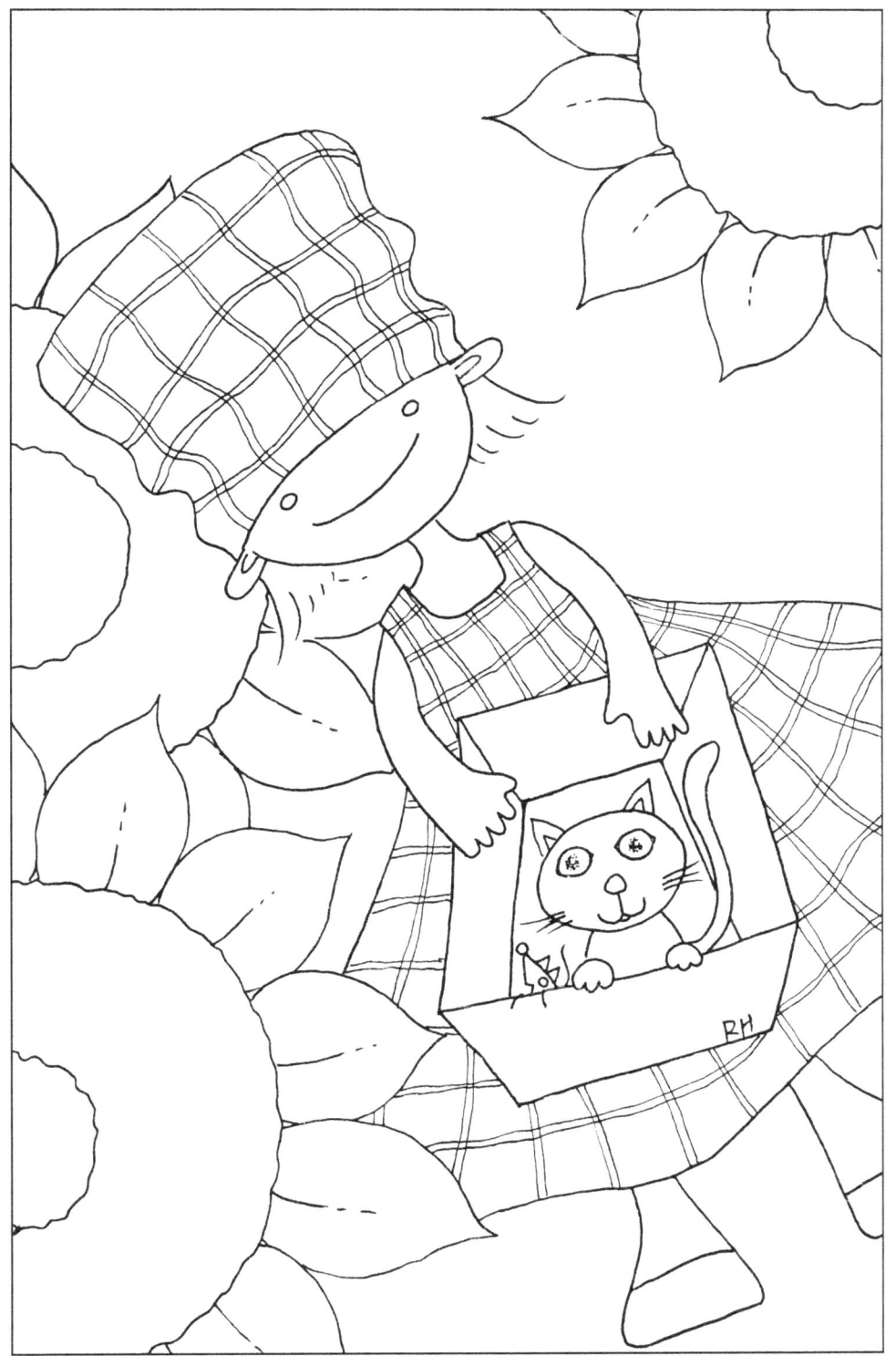

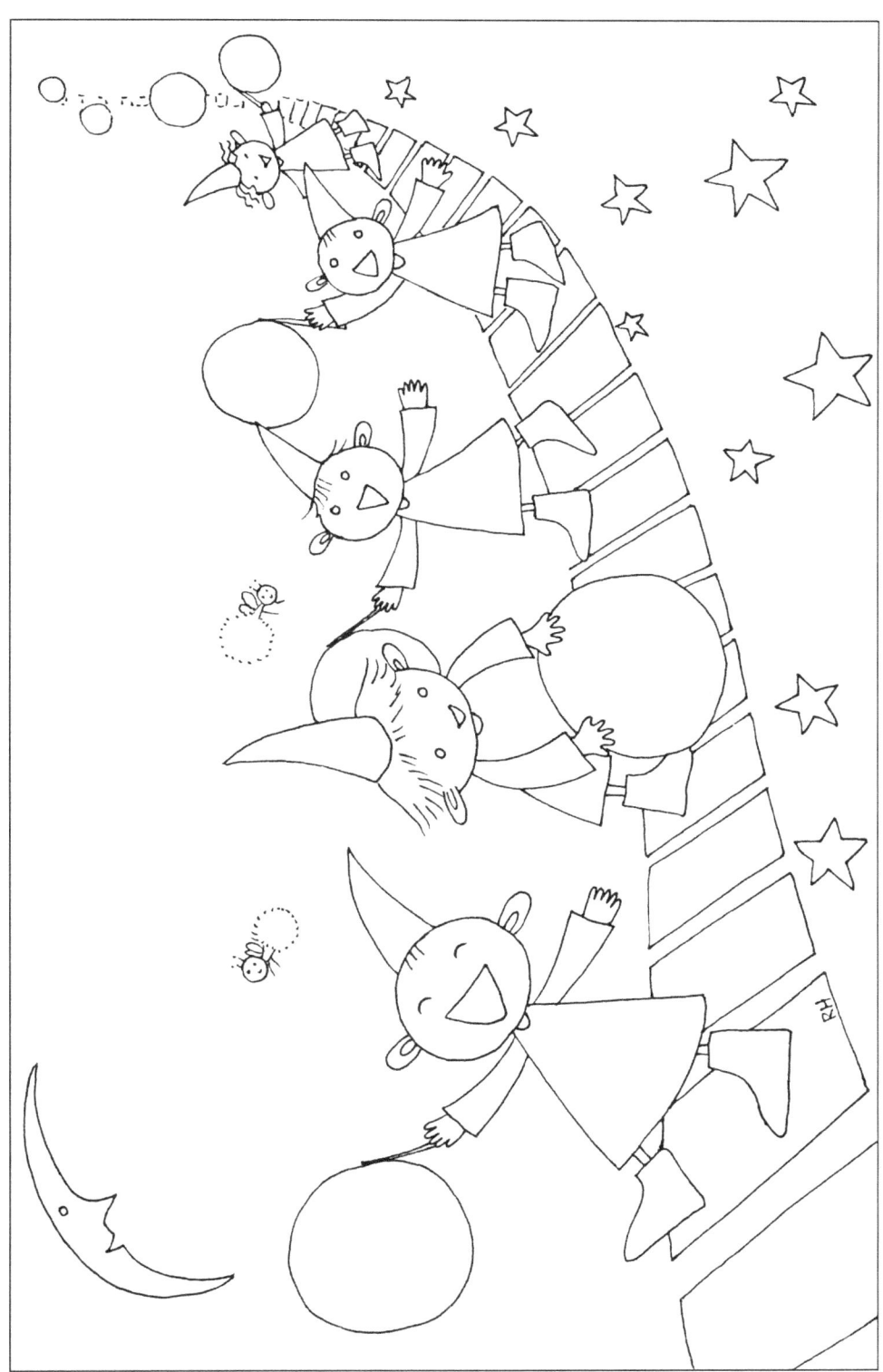

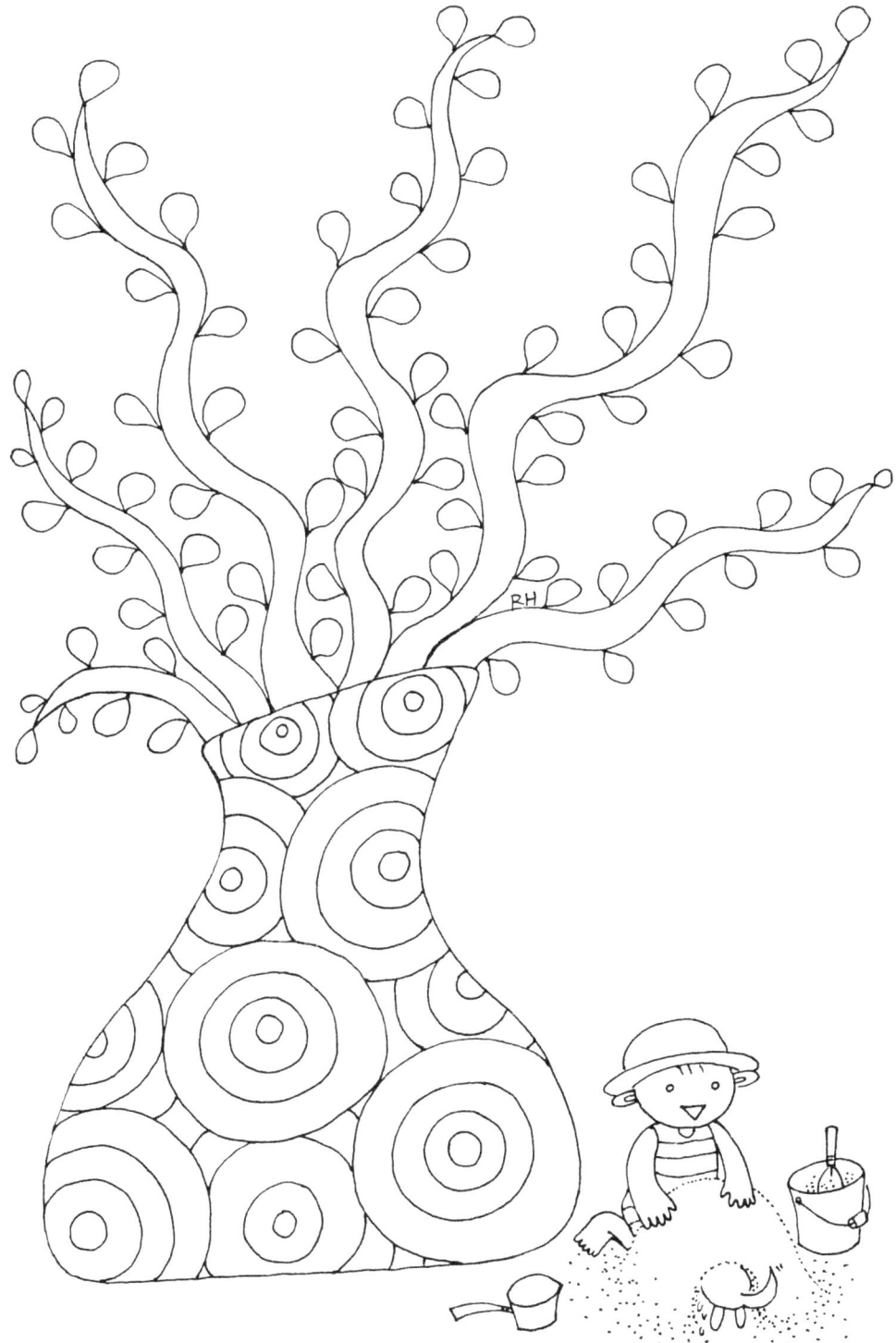

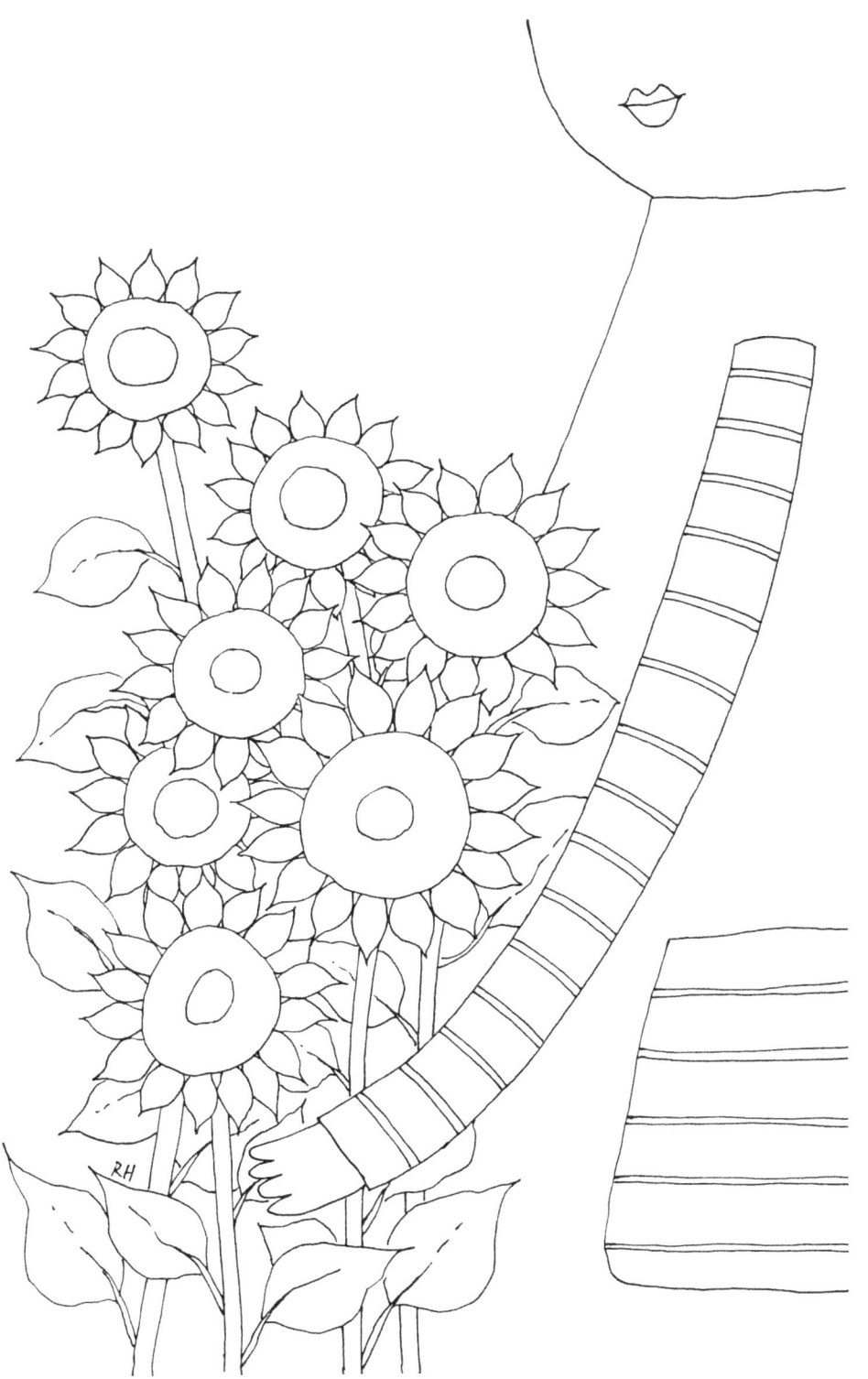

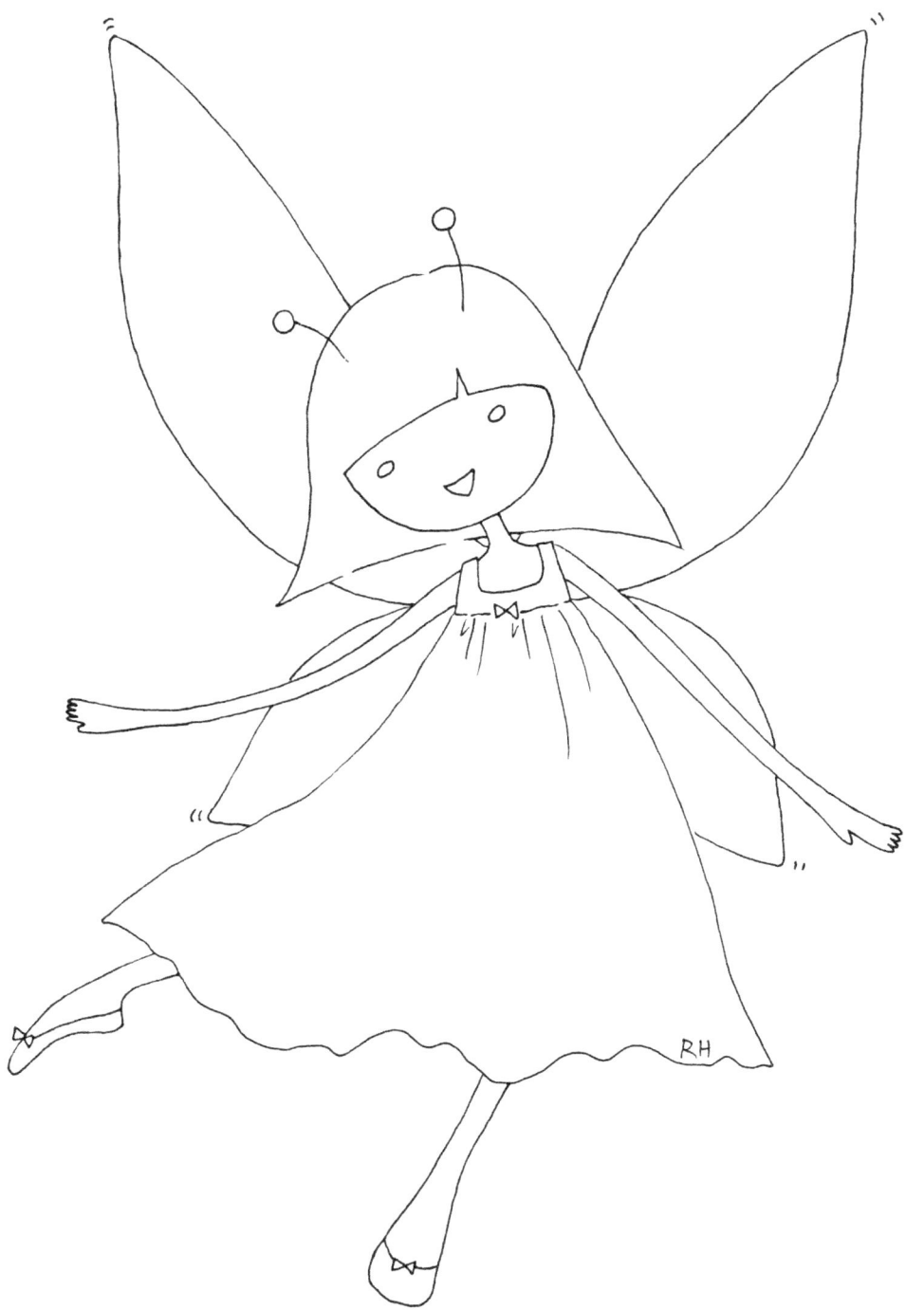

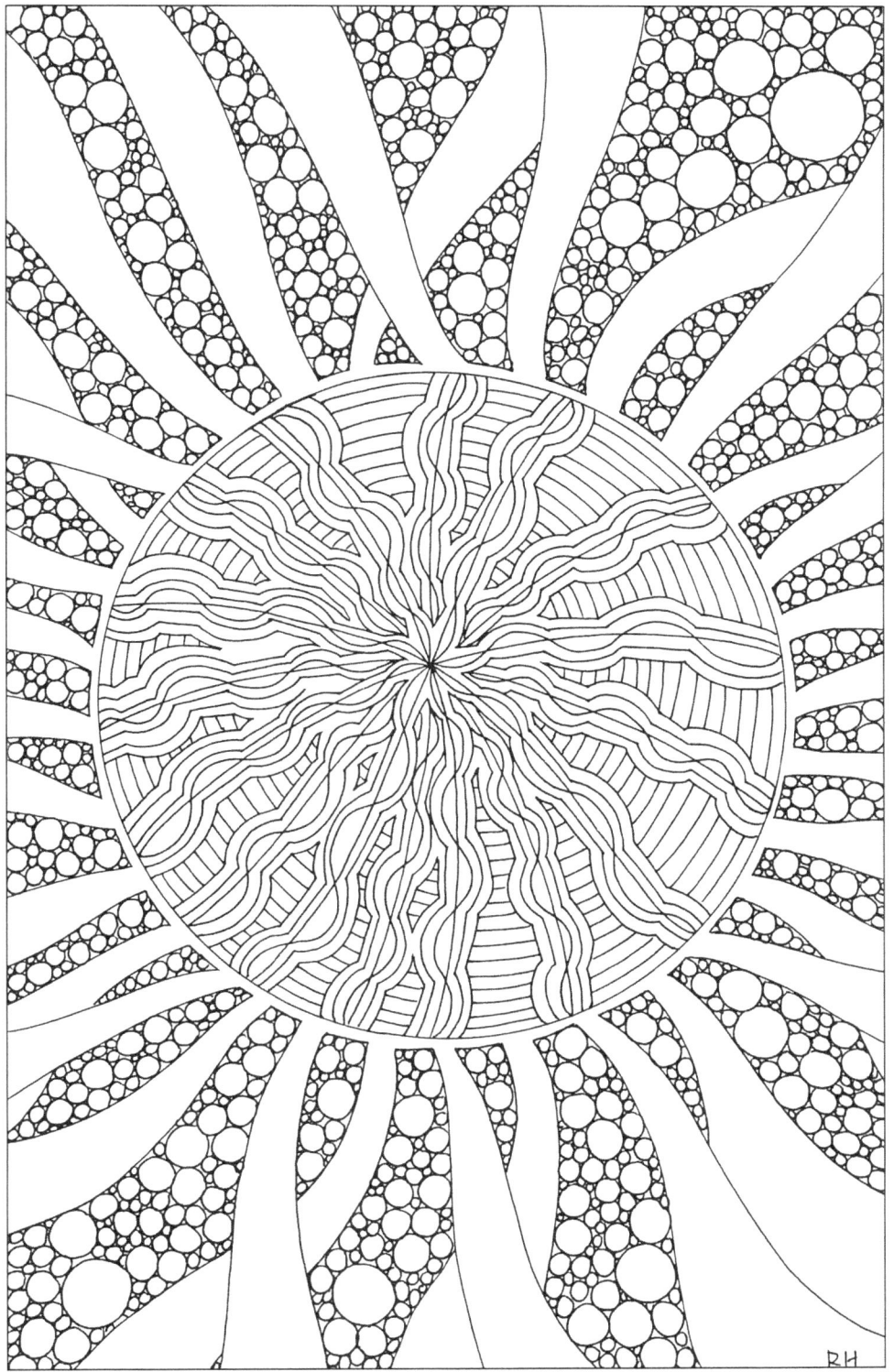

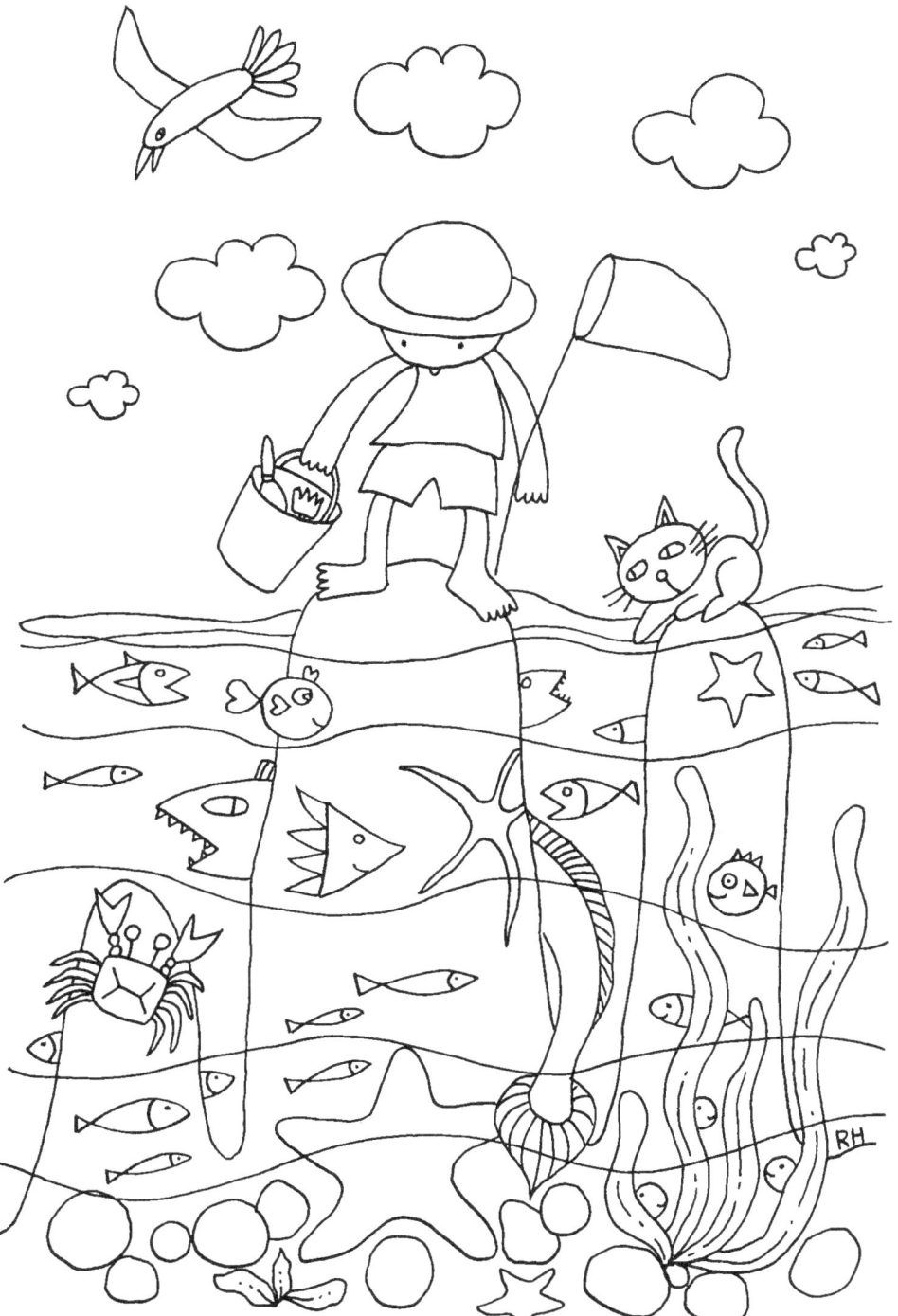

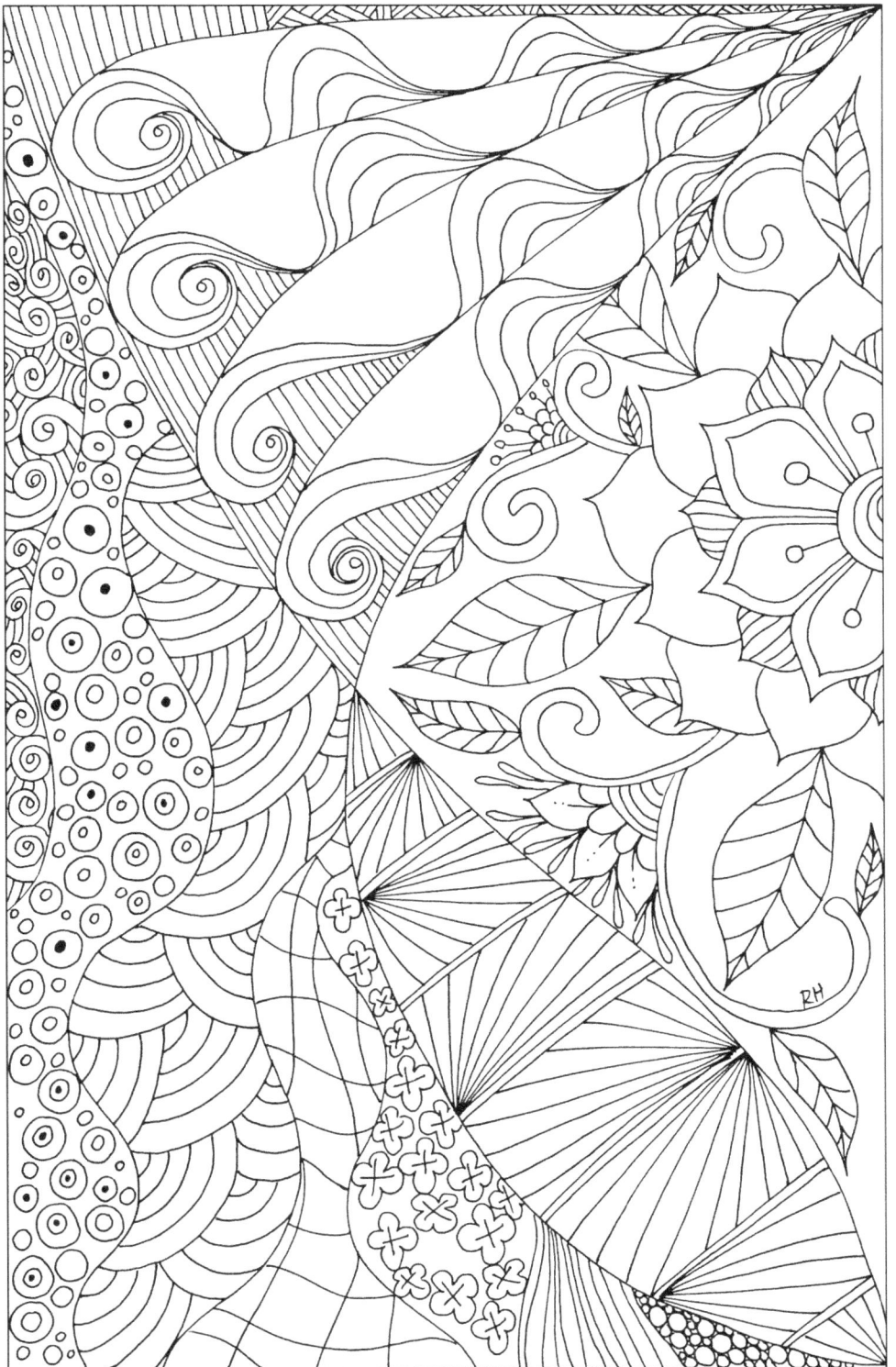

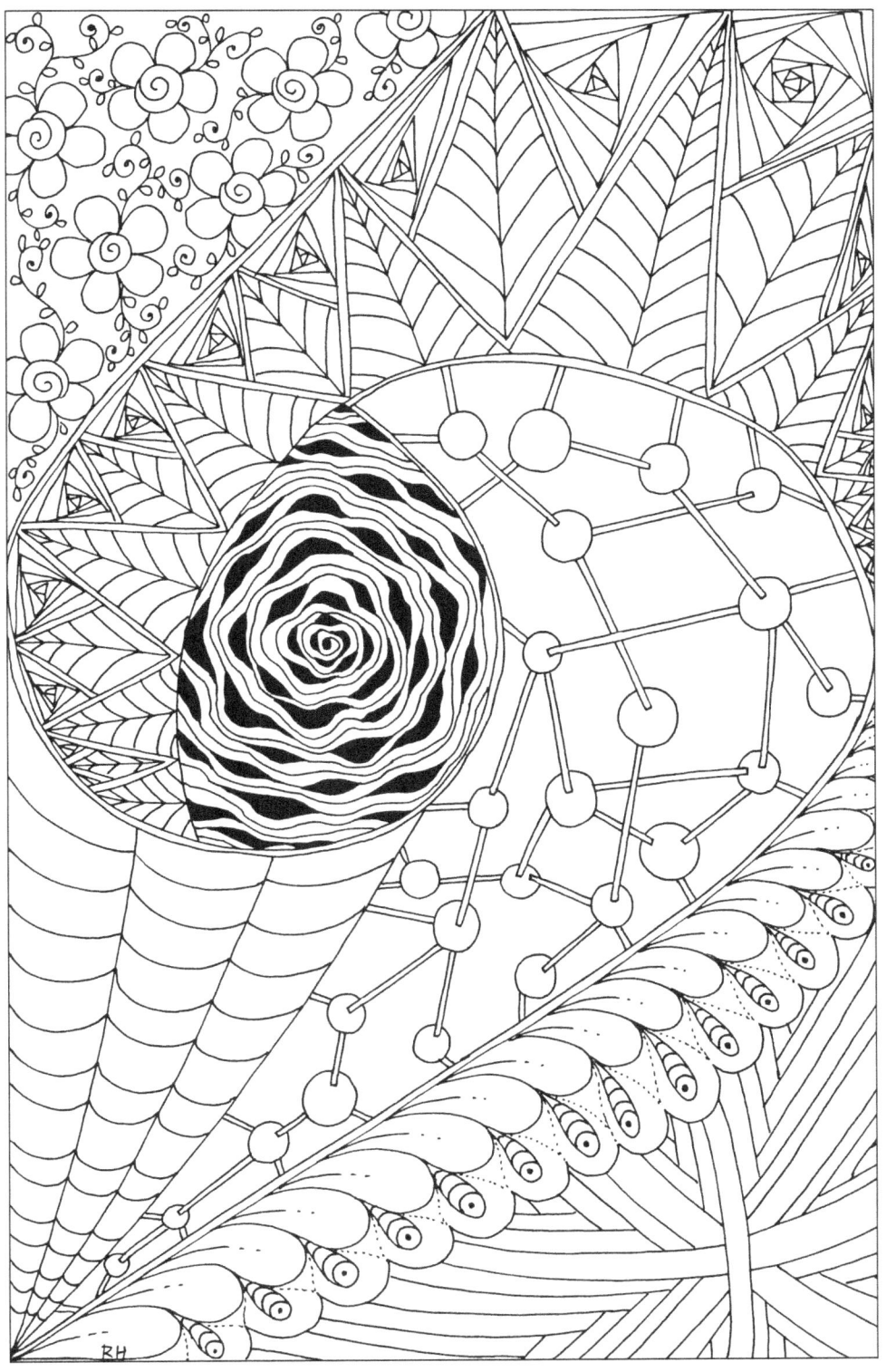

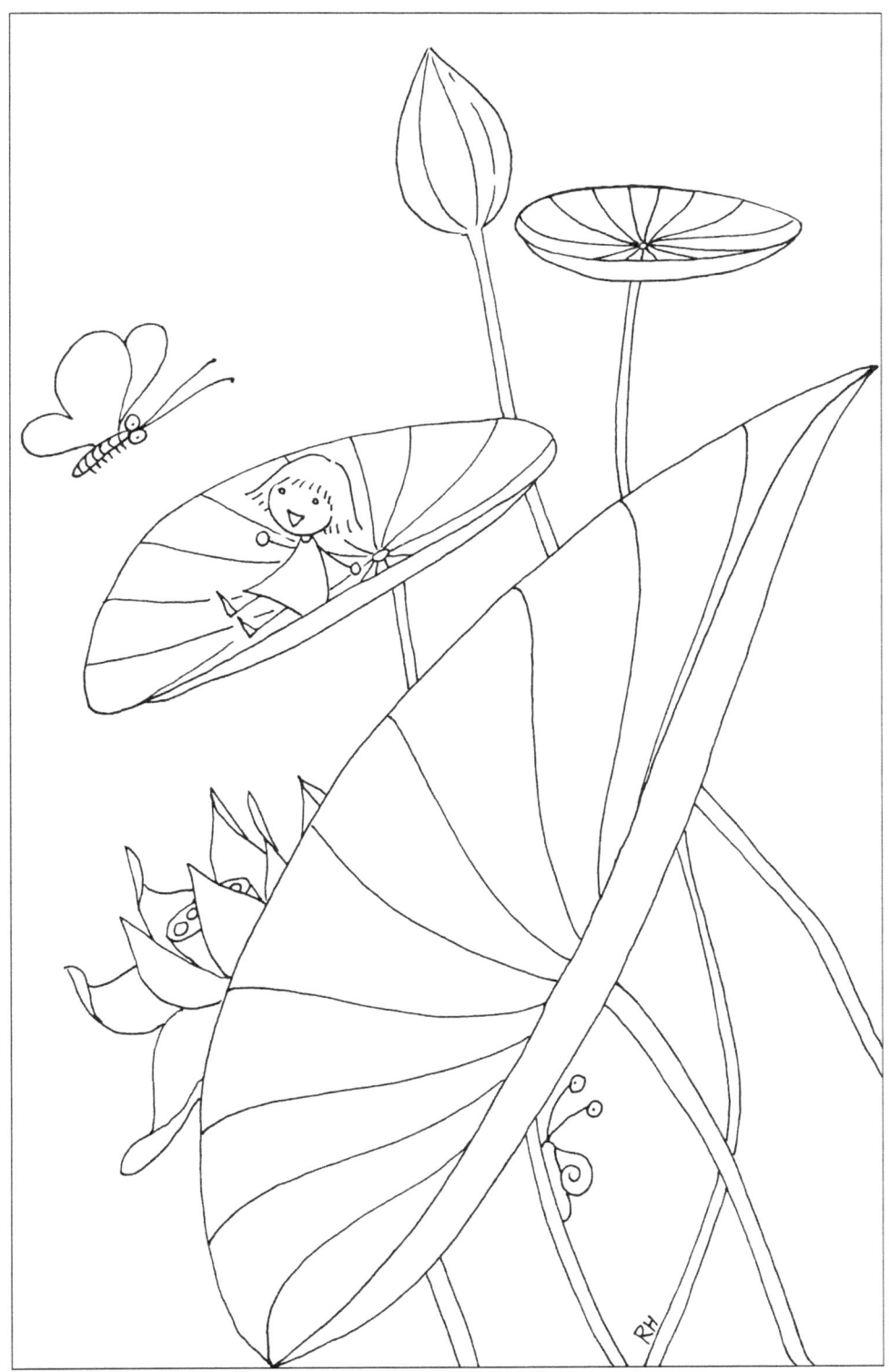

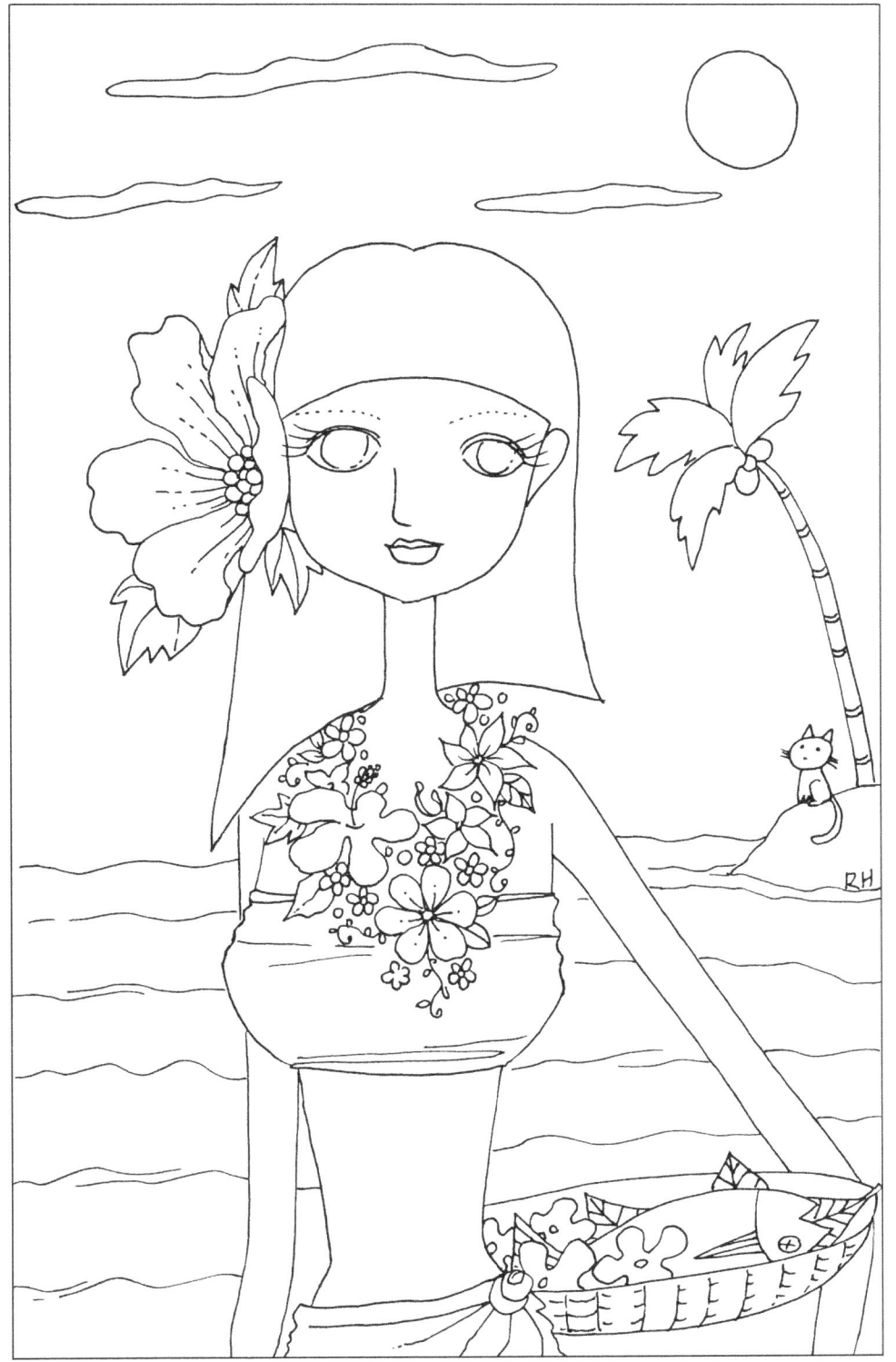

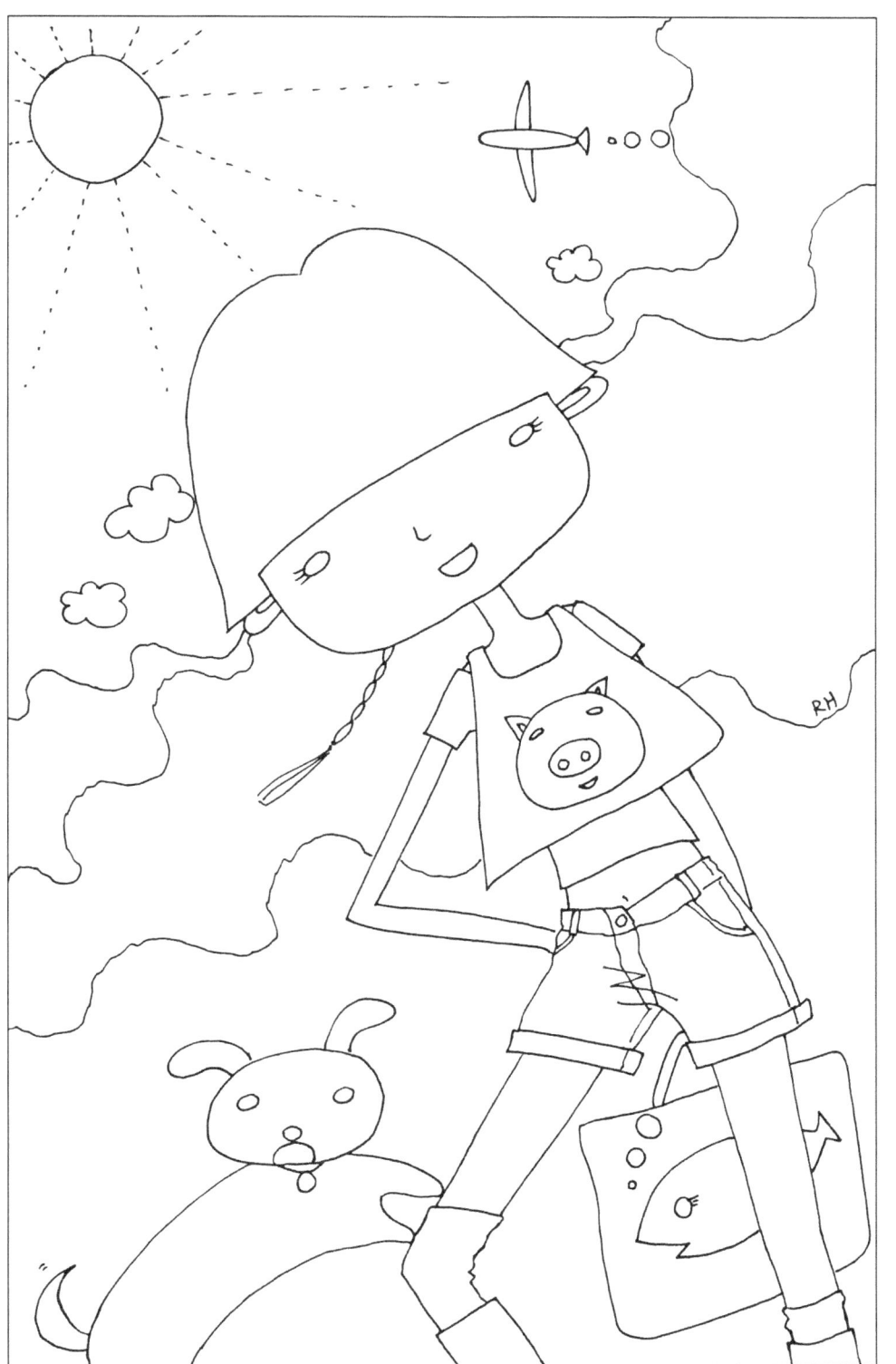

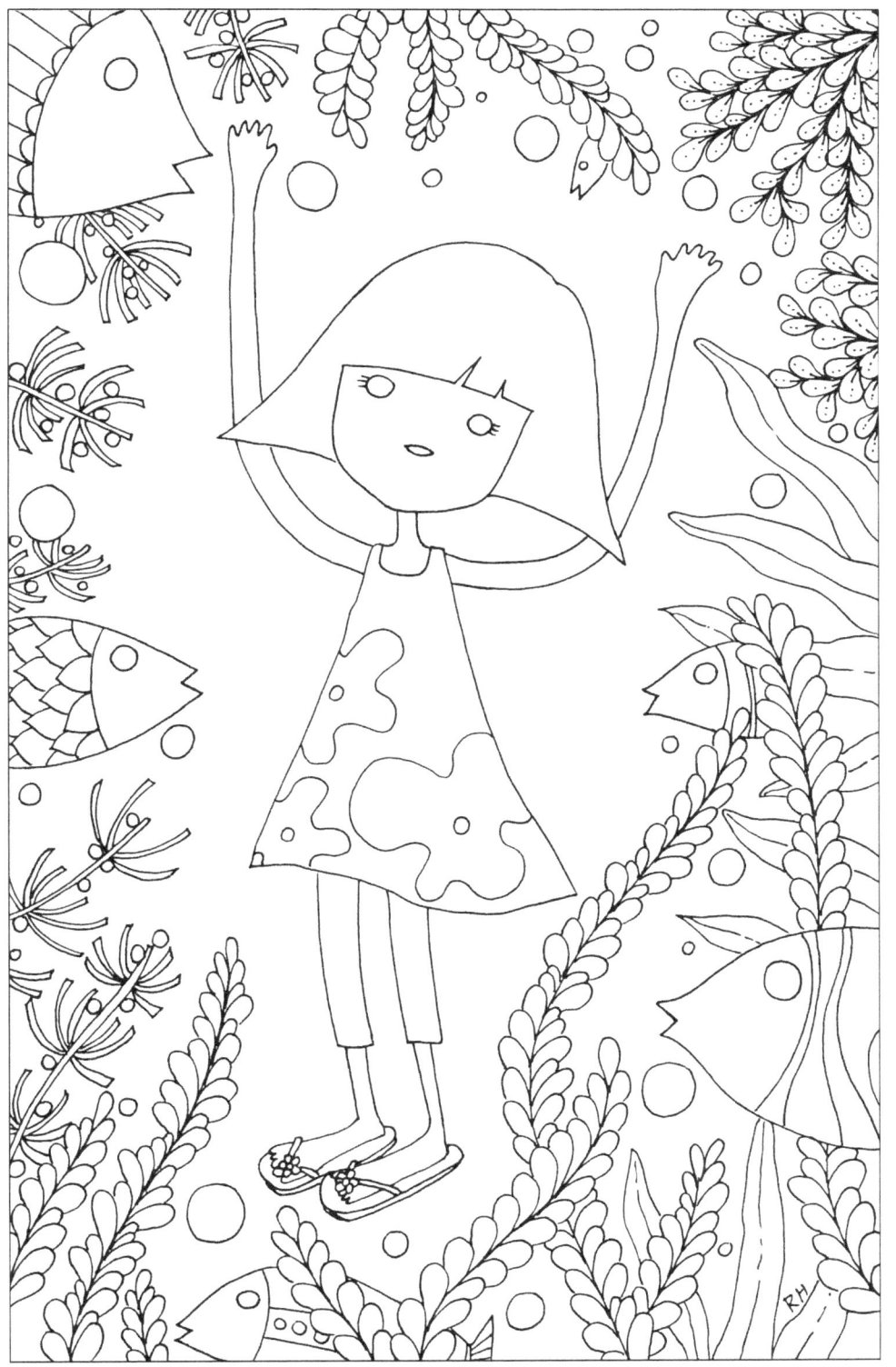

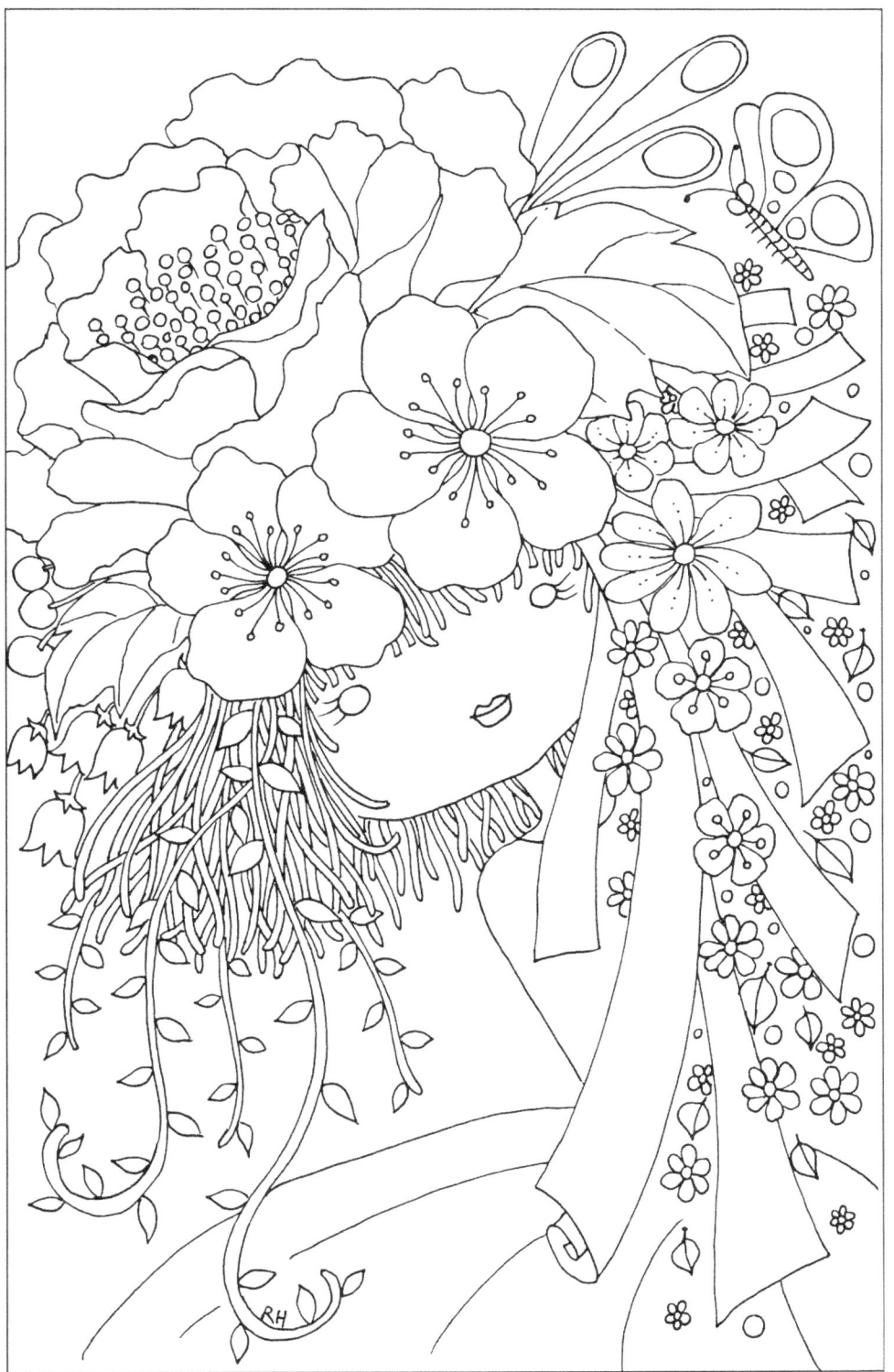

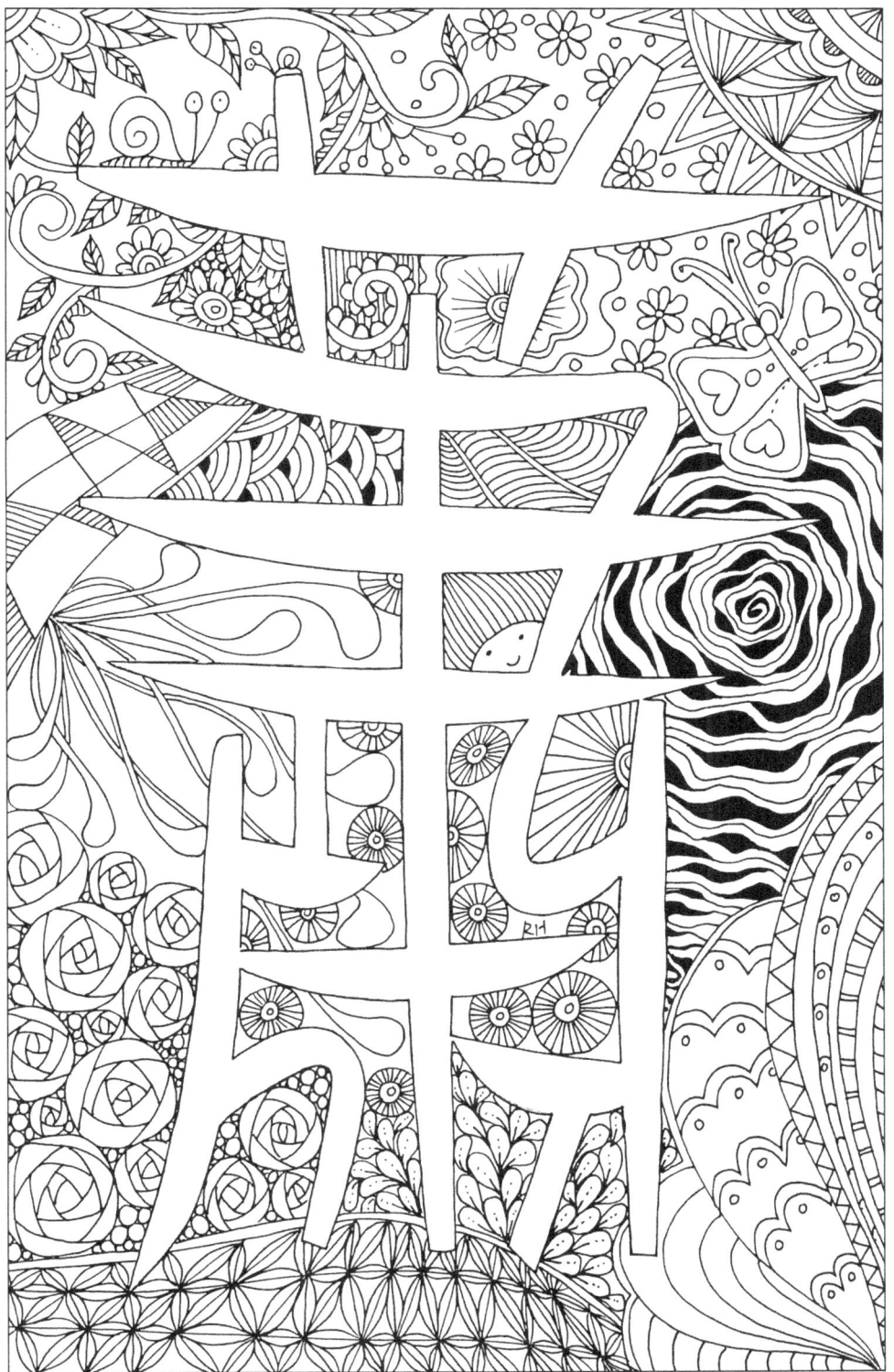

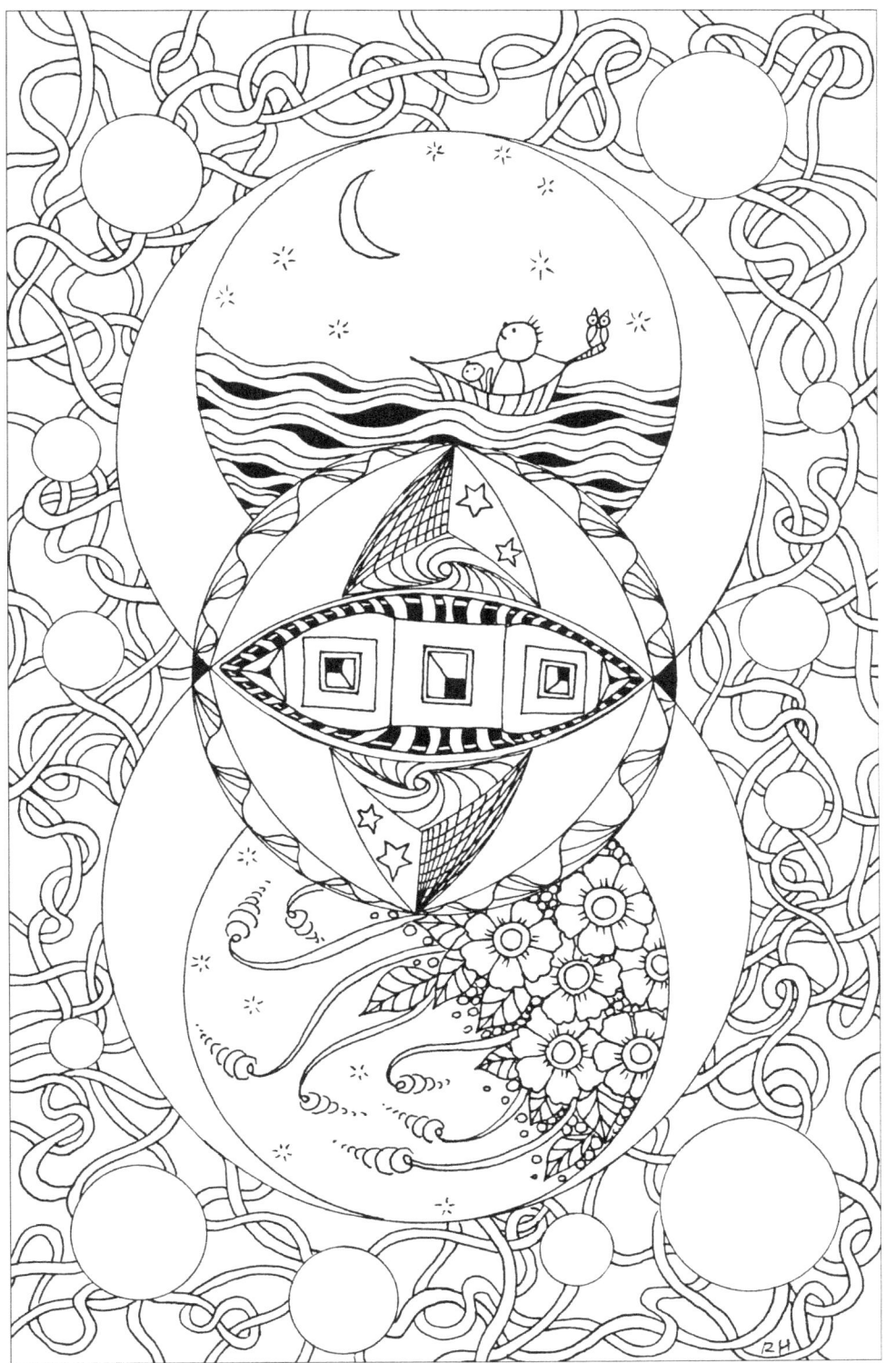

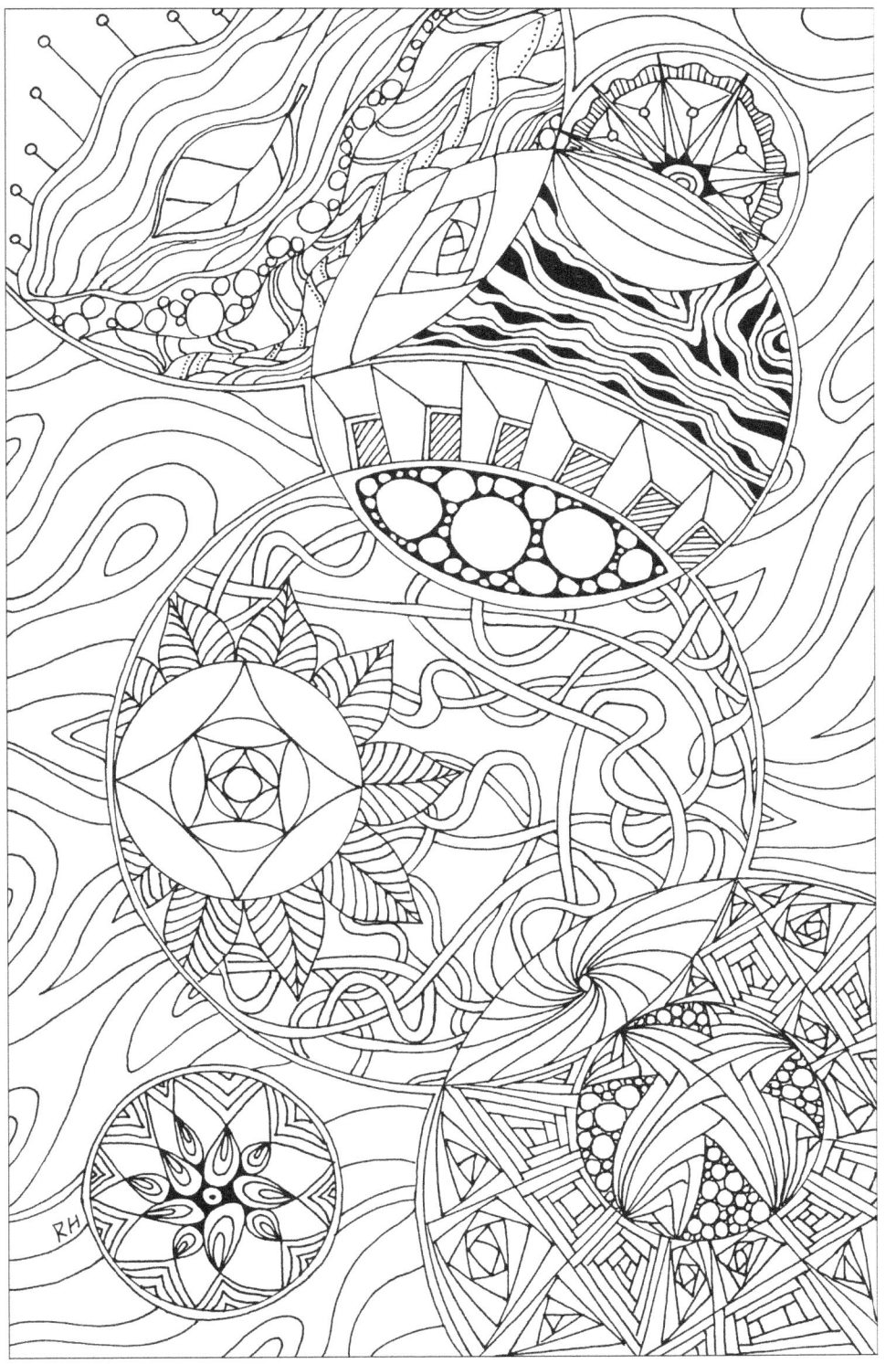

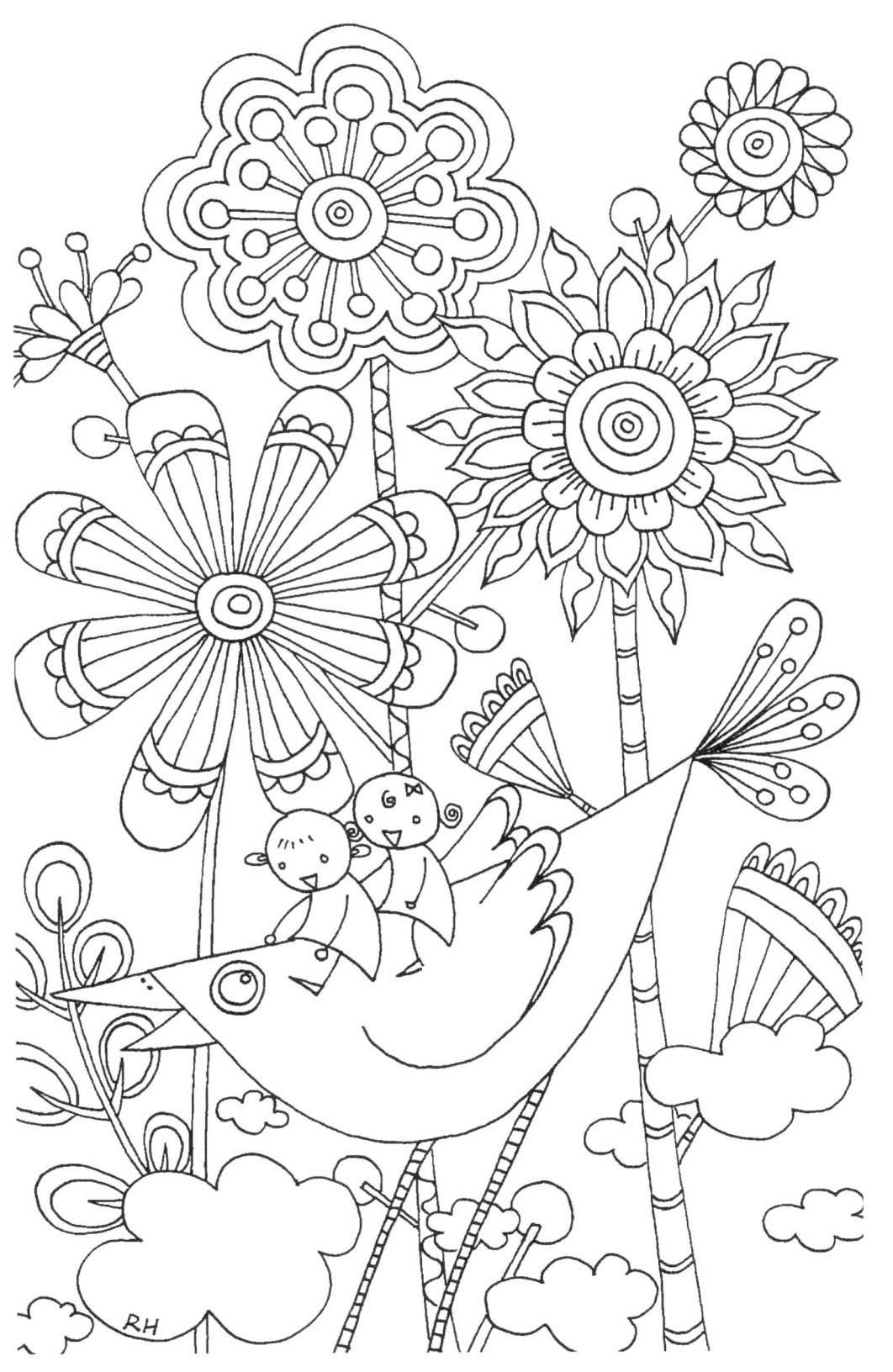

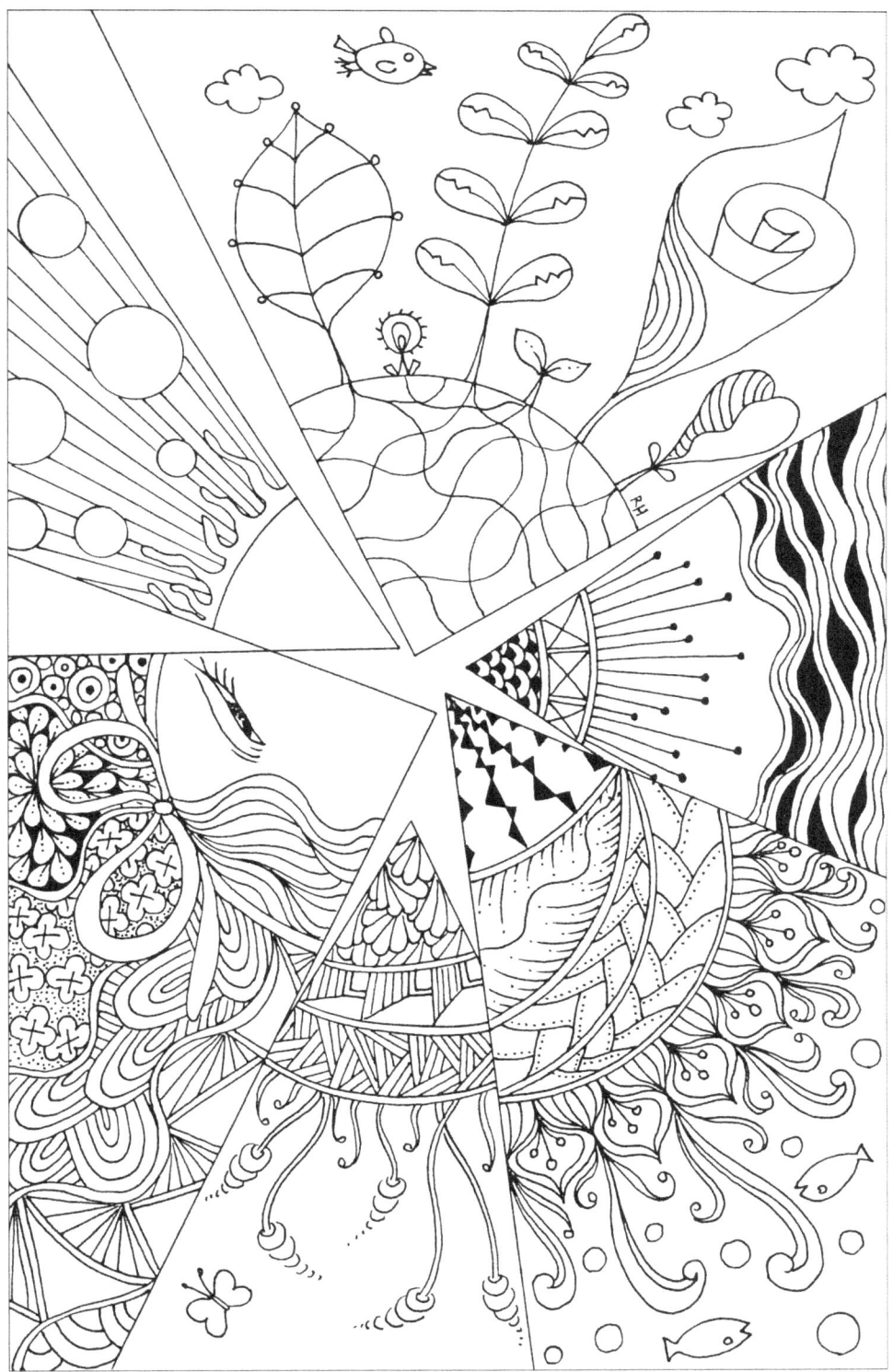

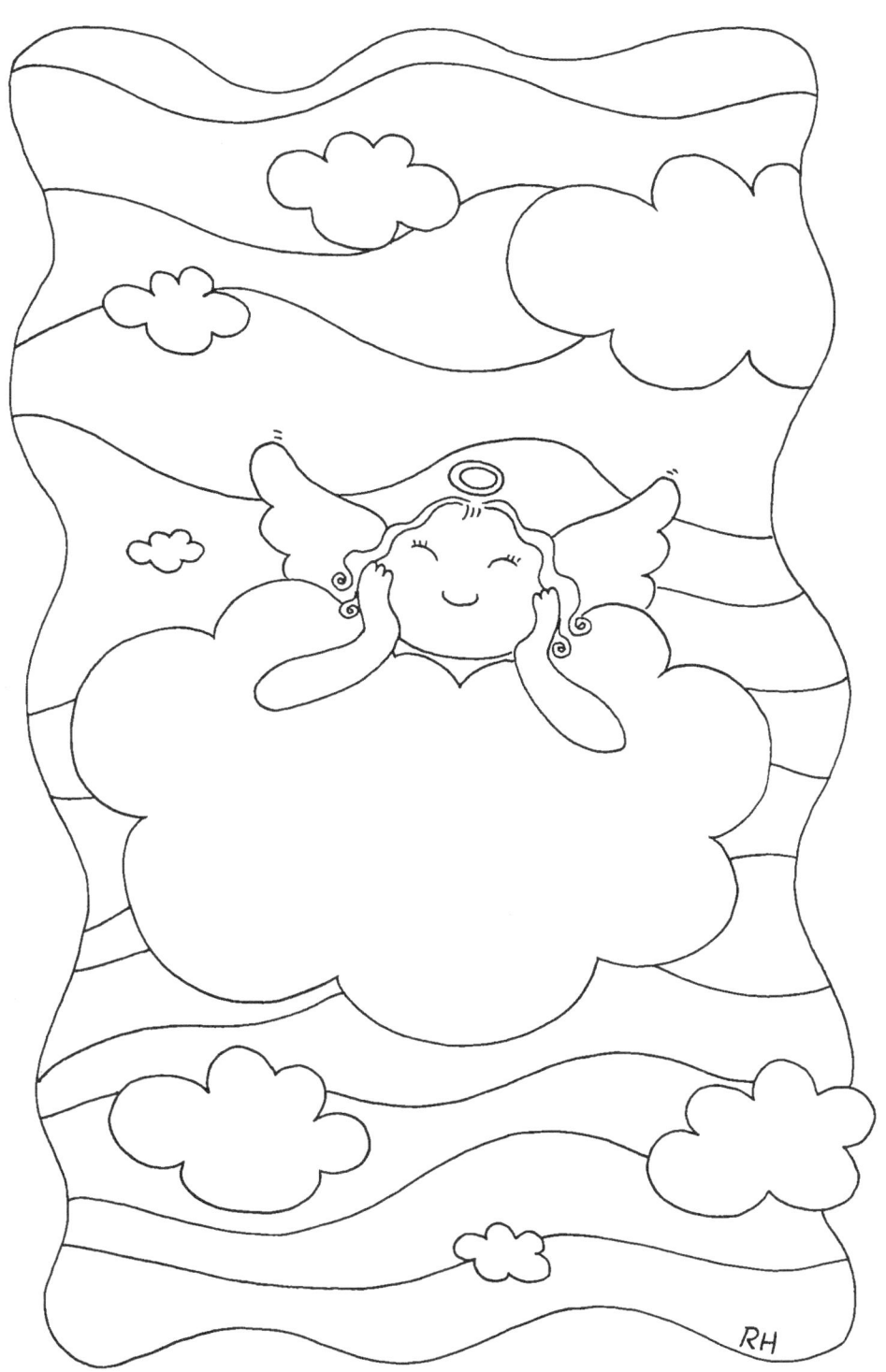

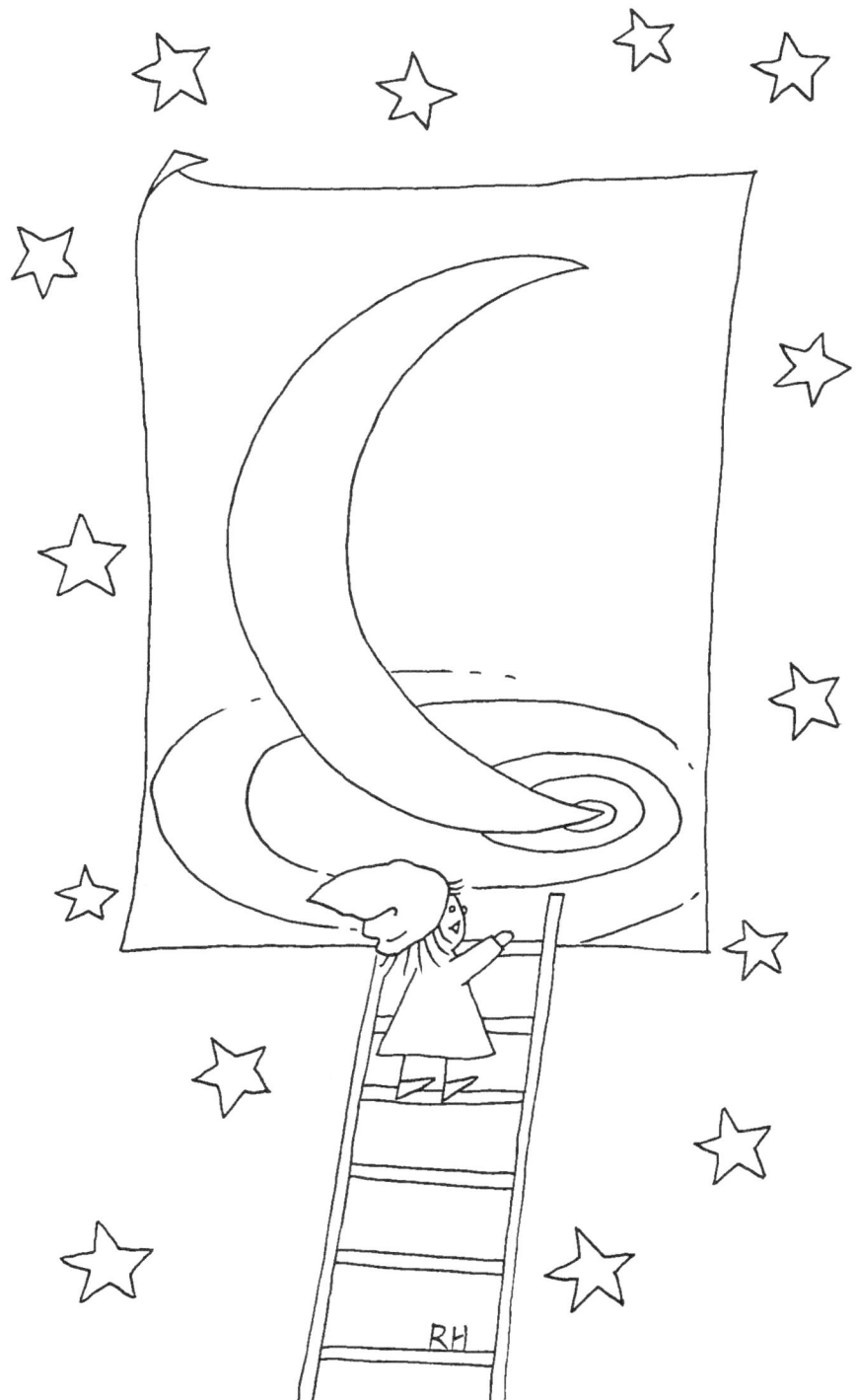

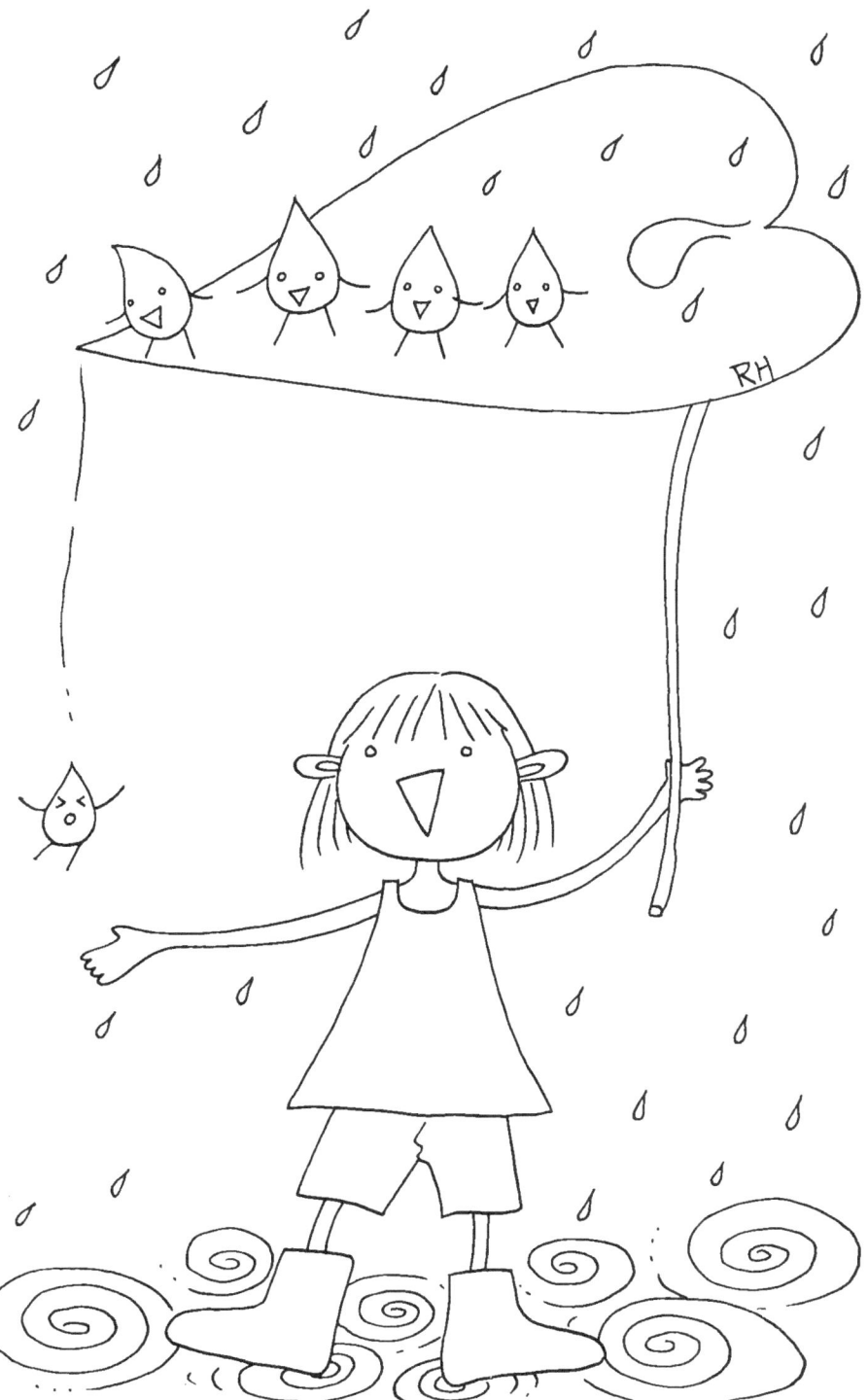

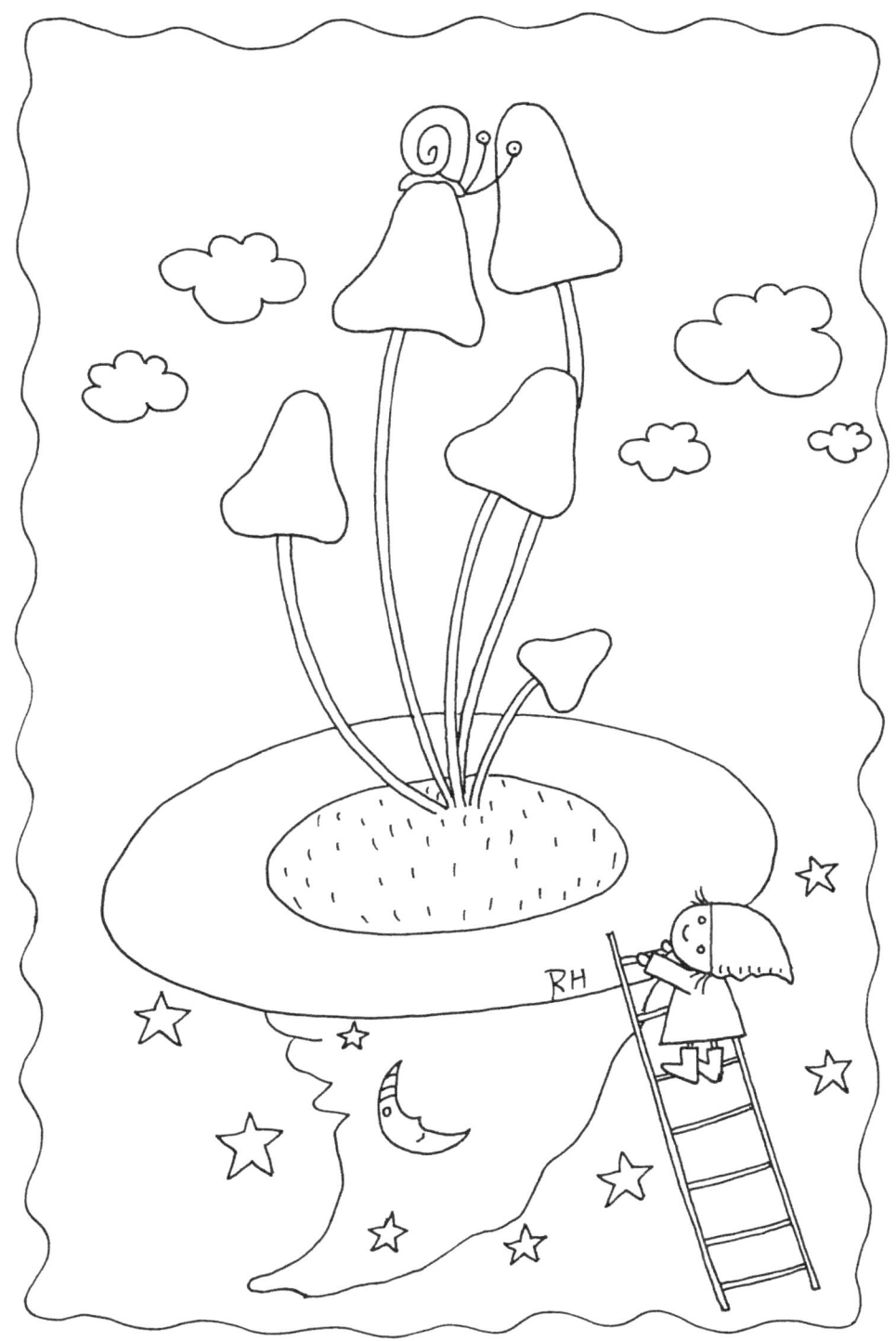

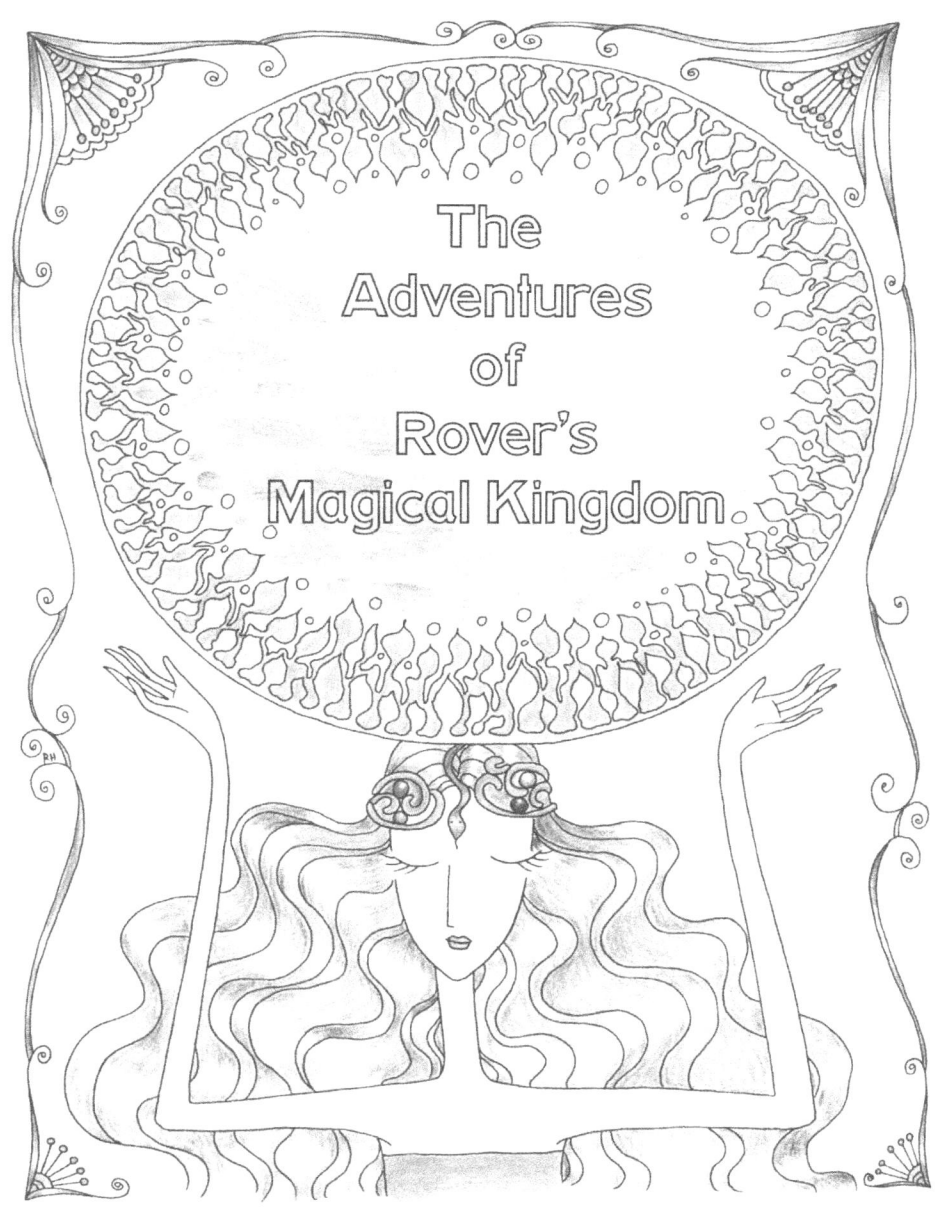

**CHECK OUT THE FIRST BOOK OF
"THE ADVENTURES OF ROVER'S
MAGICAL KINGDOM" 1
60 MAGICAL DRAWINGS**

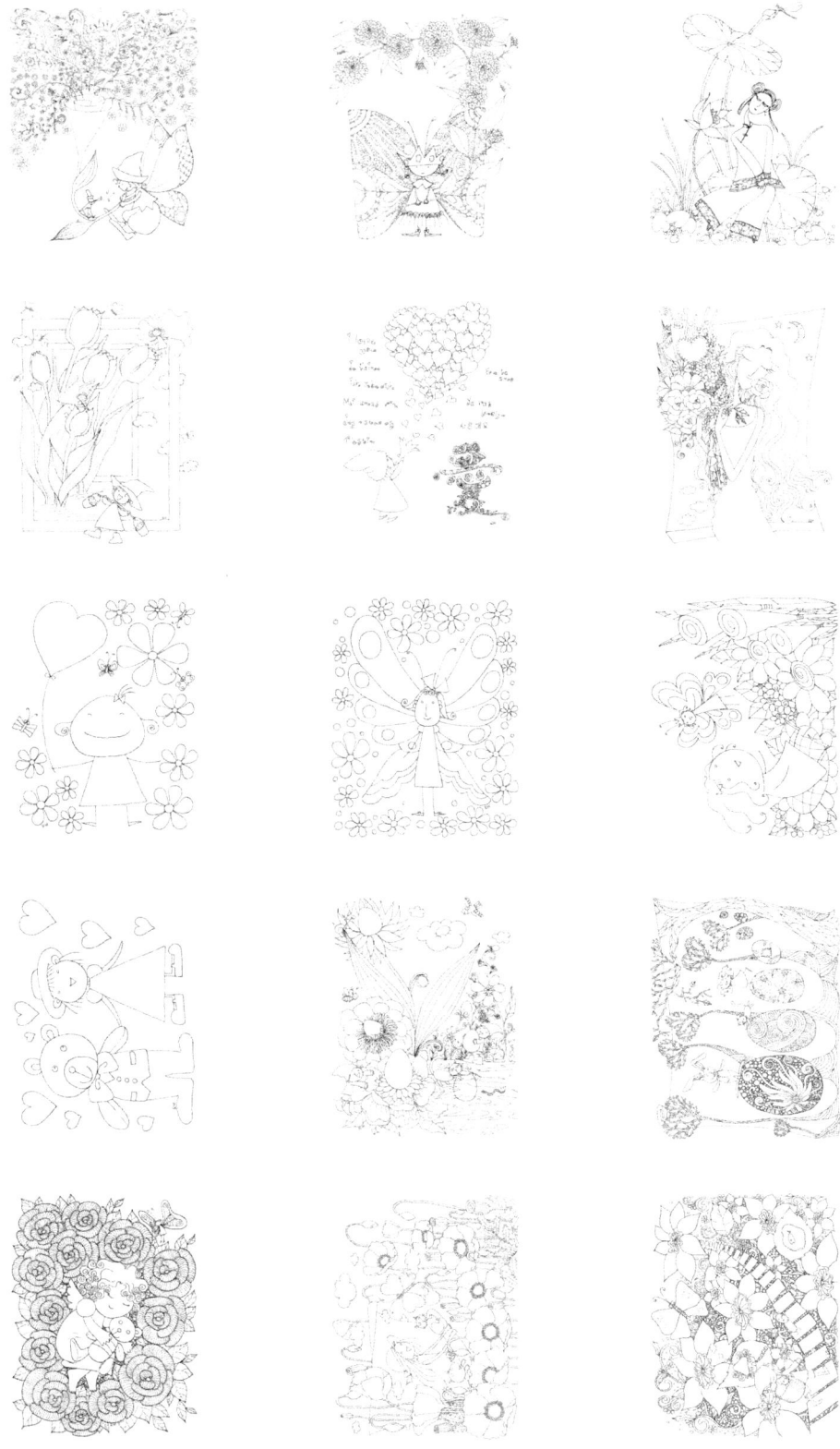

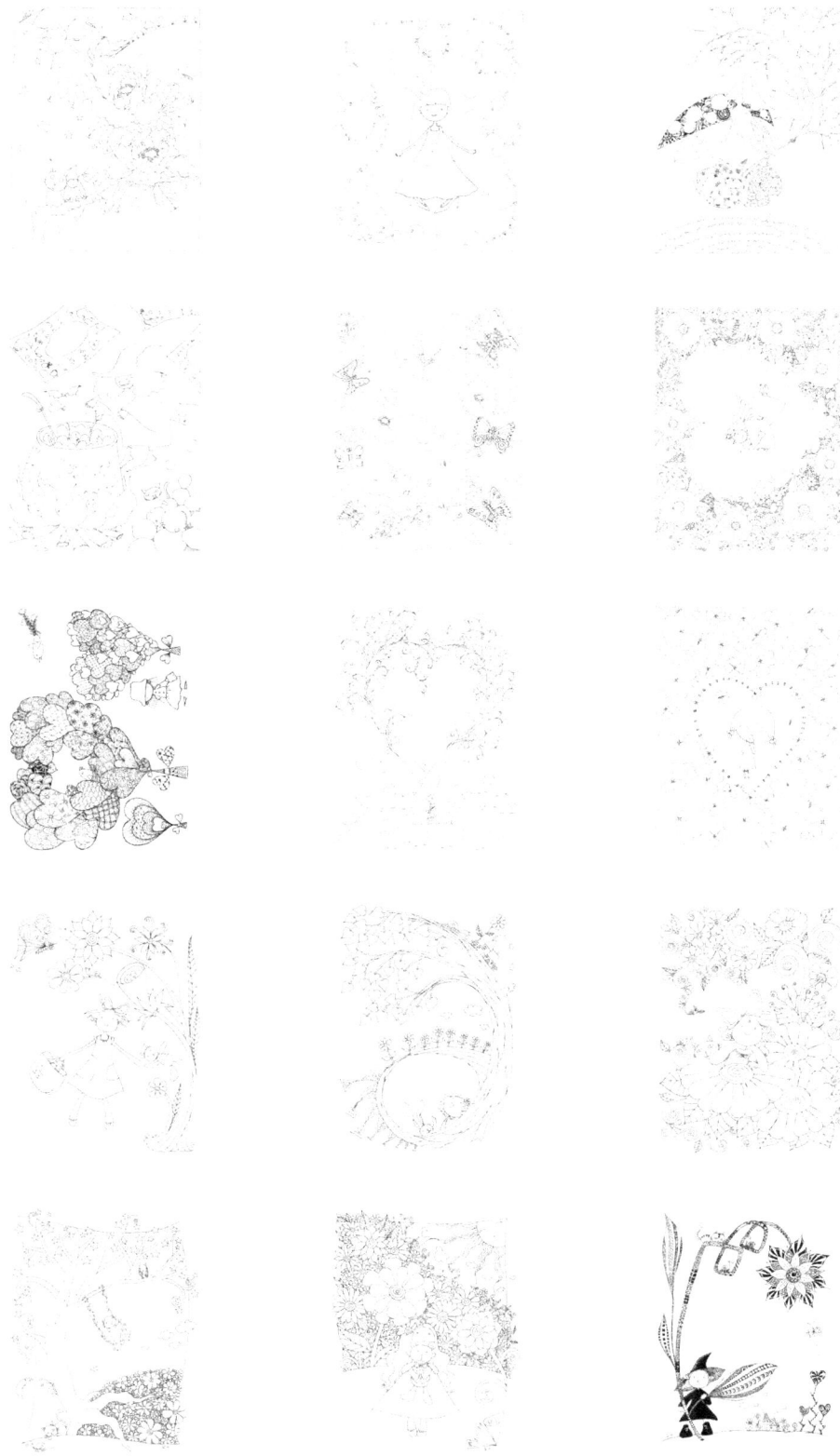

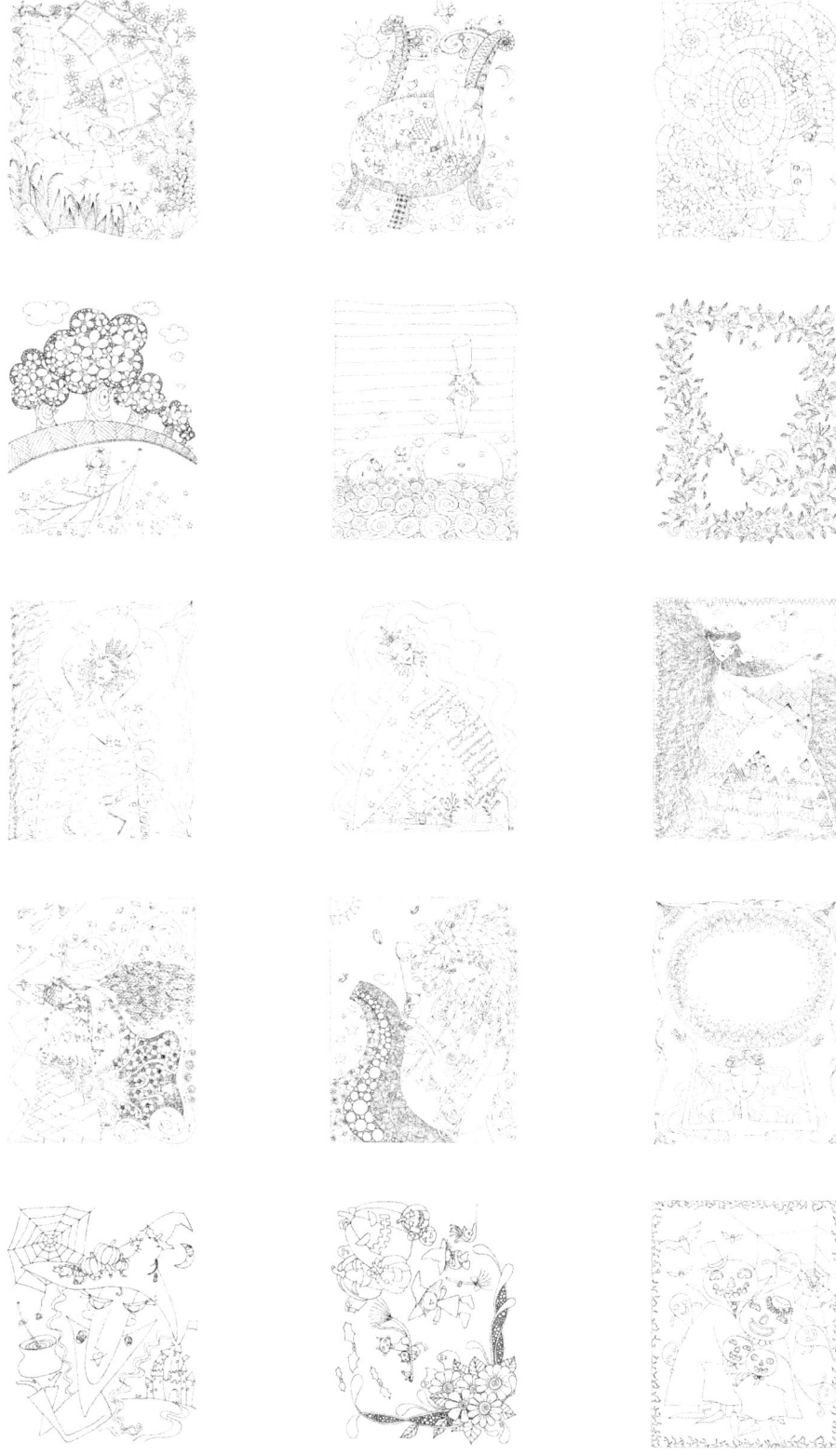

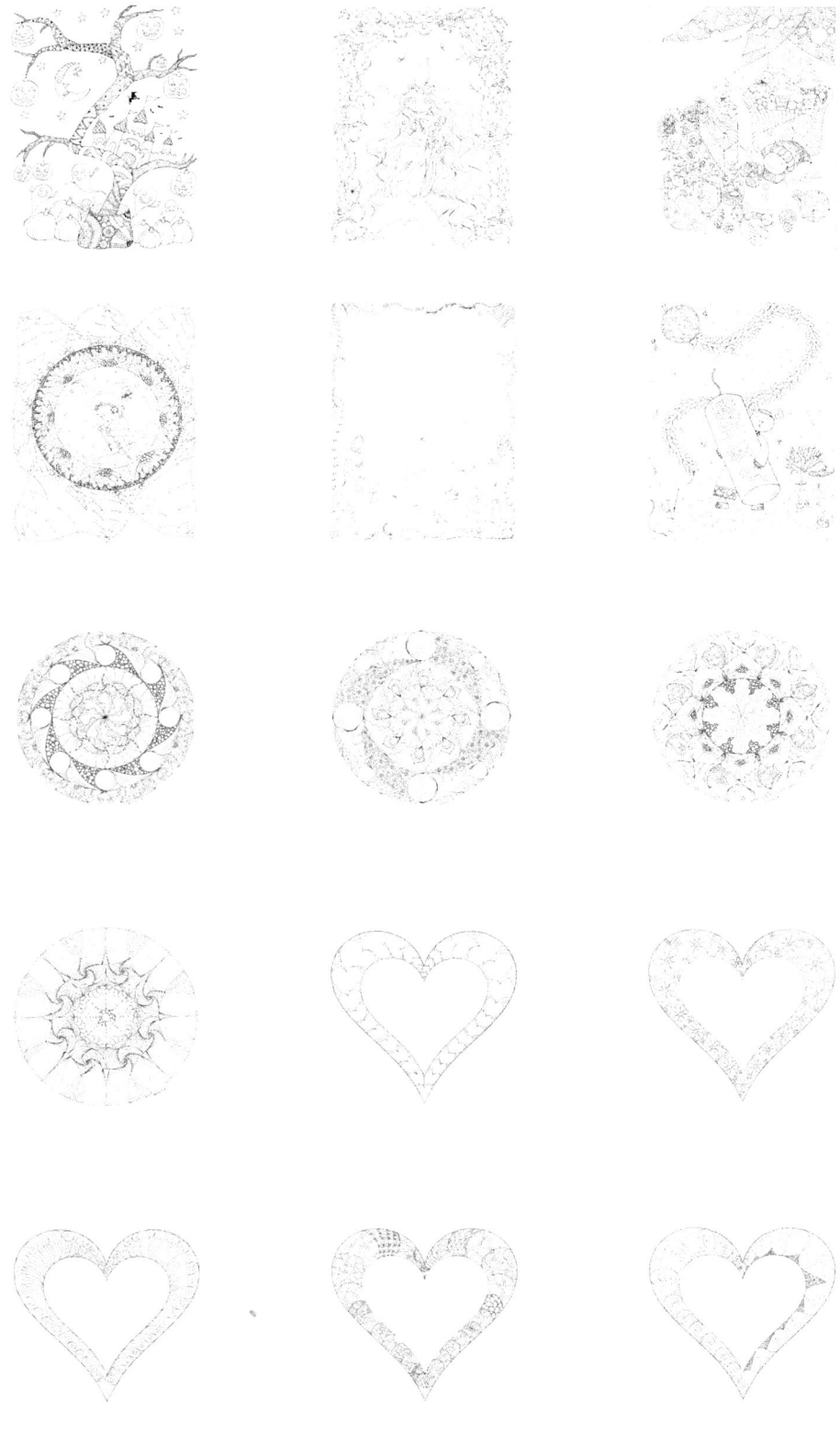

Test your colors here on the templates from

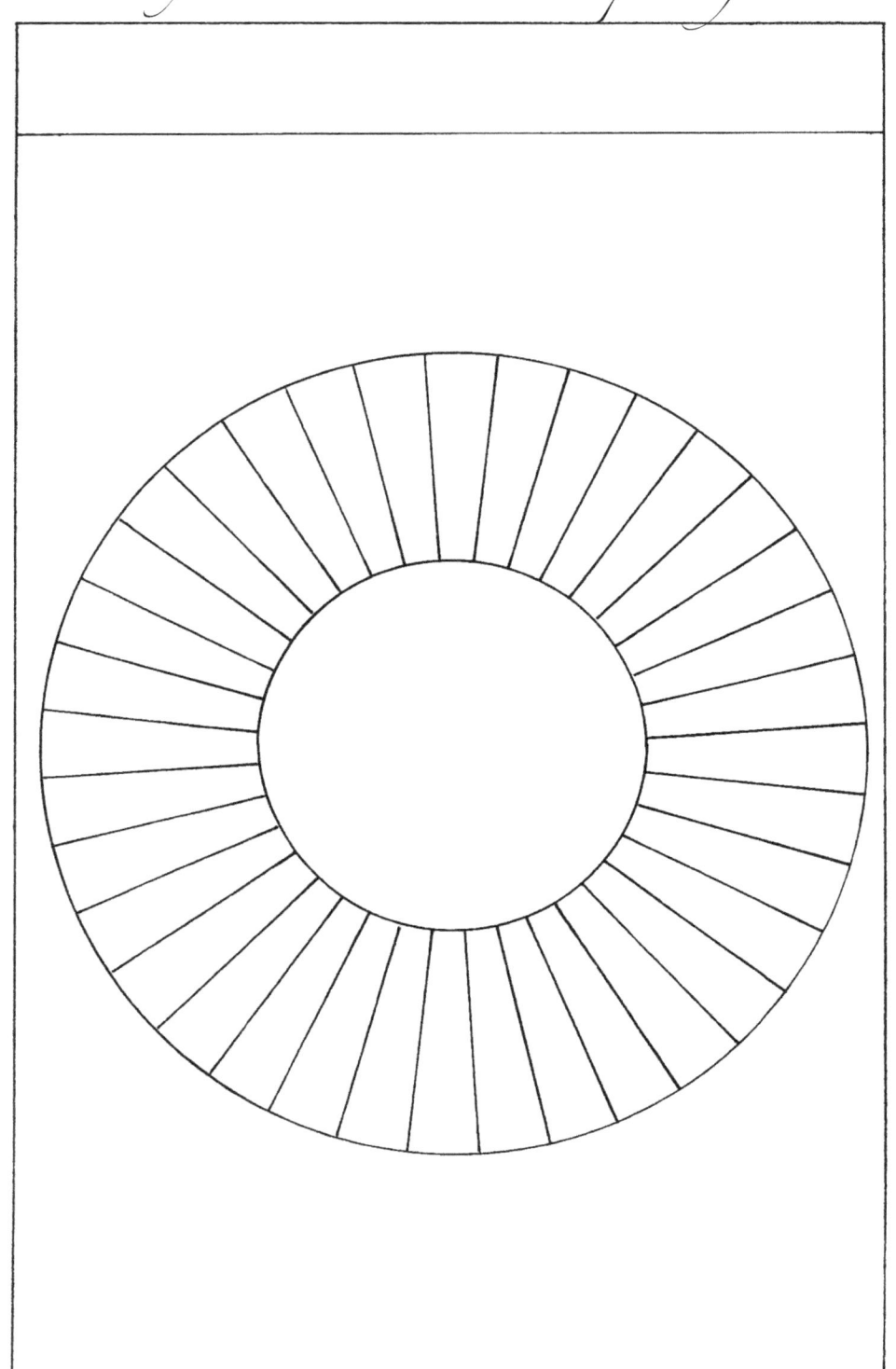

"My Pocket Coloring Companion"

www.ingramcontent.com/pod-product-compliance
Lightning Source LLC
Chambersburg PA
CBHW070302230526
45470CB00002B/689